Books Appeal

This book is dedicated to my dear aunt,
Edith Kingsley Cornell;
my favorite uncle,
Gilbert Harper Cornell;
and to my most loving parents,
William Lansing Cornell and *Marion Cornell*

Books Appeal

Get Teenagers into the School Library

by
Karen Cornell Gomberg

McFarland & Company, Inc., Publishers
Jefferson, North Carolina, and London

Cover illustration © 1987 by Jackie Urbanovic.

Library of Congress Cataloguing-in-Publication Data

Gomberg, Karen Cornell.
Books appeal.

Includes index.
1. Junior high school libraries — Activity programs.
2. High school libraries — Activity programs.
3. Youth — Books and reading.
4. Public relations — Libraries.
5. Library exhibits.
I. Title.
Z675.S3G565   1987   027.8'223   86-43224

ISBN 0-89950-255-5 (sewn softcover; acid-free natural paper)

Printed in the United States of America.

McFarland & Company, Inc., Publishers
Box 611, Jefferson, North Carolina 28640

Table of Contents

Introduction

Books Appeal: Get Teenagers into the School Library is a sequel to *Back to Books: 200 Library Activities to Encourage Reading* (by Karen Marshall). I developed *Back to Books* ... while working with elementary school children, grades K–8. *Books Appeal* was produced from my experience as a library media specialist in a junior high school, grades 7–8.

Liven up your media center, and make for more enjoyable learning and research. Generate excellent publicity and public relations. Devise games and activities to use with your students. It is fun, and the enthusiasm will reward you time and time again.

Books Appeal was written to fill a need of junior high school librarians and teachers for material to support them in activating an interest in reading for pure pleasure, as well as developing research and library skills. It is comprised of seven categories of activities: (1) Contests and Active Games; (2) Banquets, Fairs, Parties and Programs; (3) Bulletin Board Activities; (4) Fun with Book Lists; (5) Reference Books; (6) Quiet Mental Games; and (7) Displays, Projects and Exhibits.

Some of the activities in the seven categories may overlap. Some were used in *Back to Books* and are now geared for older children. Many of these activities may be adapted for elementary or high school use as well.

Success of the library program is evidenced by the heavy use of the media center by the students and teachers bringing their classes to the library. Our reference section is substantially used by students, and the sheer number of books being circulated speaks for itself.

Delight in these games and activities, and continue to devise your own.

Part I

Contests and Active Games

1. Authors Card Game

I played this game as a little girl and loved it. It was my introduction to some of the classic authors and their books. It continues to be enjoyed by children today.

The objective is to get as many "books" as possible. A "book" consists of four matching author cards, all Mark Twain, for example. A player asks an opponent if he holds a specific title by a particular author. If the opponent does, he must relinquish it to the player who asks for it.

The library media specialist should possess four to five packs of "Authors" if using the game with a class. A dummy set can be made by mimeographing photographs of twelve chosen authors from the *Junior Book of Authors* series. The five volumes include: *Junior Book of Authors* — Stanley J. Kunitz & Howard Haycraft, eds. *More Junior Authors* — Muriel Fuller, ed. *Third Book of Junior Authors* — Doris de Montreville & Donna Hill, eds. *Fourth Book of Junior Authors & Illustrators* — Doris de Montreville & Elizabeth Crawford, eds. *Fifth Book of Junior Authors & Illustrators* — Sally Holtze, ed. The publisher of these volumes is the H.W. Wilson Co.

Type four titles by each author on each "card," alternating the title at the top. (The title at the top is considered that card's "title.") Duplicate the cards on the copier. If you want these cards to survive, have your library aides back each one with oak tag. You will be able to keep them for some time. Select well-known authors who have written at least four titles.

2. Genre Flash

Post a list of fiction genres for the group to see: science fiction; historical fiction; romance; fantasy; adventure; teenage contemporary; classics; etc. The library media specialist may hold up fifteen to twenty titles for the group to see. Students must determine to which genre the title belongs. First correct answer wins; points may be assigned for each winning answer. English classes may compete for the highest score.

3. Dewey Flash

Make visible the Dewey Decimal System of Classification by posting it on the bulletin board or the side of the bookcase or by passing out dittos. The library media specialist then photocopies fifteen to twenty pages from various nonfiction books (one page from each book), including various Dewey classes. Students try to decide the Dewey class from which each photocopied page was taken.

4. City Chase

The social studies class may enjoy participating in this race. The class is divided into two to four units. One person of each group will be group secretary; he or she is given a piece of paper and a pencil. The librarian or teacher chooses the name of a well-known city or town in the world, and the students try to think of a city or town that is located in a specified direction from the city or town given. For example: "Write down the name of a city or town that lies east of Paris." Students confer within their groups; each student in the group must give an answer, and the group secretary writes the answers down.

After each student in each group has completed the task, the answers are checked by the teacher, librarian, and the group secretary. Questions as to accuracy of answers can be checked in any atlas and in *Webster's Geographical Dictionary* (G. & C. Merriam Co.). The group that completes first with the most correct answers wins.

5. Aquarium Aesthetics

Under the auspices of the science department, student aides at our school are trained to care for the fifty-gallon freshwater aquarium placed in our library. Aquarium maintenance and fish identification are part of our science curriculum. Students have a never-ending interest in this beautiful attraction, and the sound of water filtering through the pump is remarkably soothing and relaxing. This gorgeous tank really complements the library.

Photographs of various types of aquarium fish may be displayed on the bulletin board. Choose at least ten: for instance, the redhook metynnis; the golden albino angelfish; the orange chromide; the spotted leporinus; the zebra danio; the white convict cichlid; the paradise fish. Let students identify them. Exhibit aquarium fish reference tools nearby.

6. Spelling Bee

Sponsor a spelling bee for a specific subject of the curriculum. Arrange this with the science teacher, the history teacher, the math teacher, or any other subject teacher. A list of words peculiar to the subject could be procured from the teacher. Such an activity may be arranged after students have been exposed to the particular material. The class may be divided into two teams. Students may also be asked to give a definition of the term.

7. Links

Present ten to twenty numbered items on a table. Students are to guess what well-known personality, past or present, the object calls to mind, by linking or connecting the name of the object with the name of the personality.

1. Alexander Graham Bell. (A bell.)
2. John Audubon. (Picture of an automobile or a model of an auto plus capital of Germany.)
3. Guglielmo Marconi. (Macaroni.)

4. Jack London. (Picture of Big Ben or Buckingham Palace.)
5. Socrates. (Socks.)
6. Martin Luther King. (A card with the king.)
7. Eleanor Roosevelt. (Rose plus a piece of felt.)
8. Elizabeth Blackwell. (A black card plus a photo of a well.)
9. Jules Verne. (V plus a fern.)
10. Nellie Bly. (An illustration of a bee plus an illustration of a bird flying.)

8. Picture Perfect

English classes may enjoy this activity. The entire class may be involved with this game, or just a small group of students. The class is divided into two teams of at least three players each. The library media specialist jots down a list of five to ten fiction book titles on a piece of paper. The first person of each team is taken aside, and shown the first title. Upon returning to his team, the student must draw a picture representing the title. He may continue to draw or begin further drawings until one of his teammates identifies the book title. No one may receive verbal clues.

After a student has identified the title, he may proceed to the student captain for the next book title on the list. The team that guesses the most titles is the winner.

9. Category Charades

This activity is similar to the standard charades game. Words are chosen, however, that are included in a particular category. For instance: (1) trees — (L mm: Elm). (2) cities — (heart ford: Hartford). (3) famous biographies — (ant toe knee: Susan B. Anthony). Miming must be done by syllables. Correlate this game to any subject.

10. Verbal Charades

This game is also played in a similar manner to the standard charades except that the participants speak instead of mime scenes representing the syllables, and finally the entire word. Student players must actually say them while acting in various scenes. This game is extremely easy to play, more so than the standard charades. Again, correlate this activity to the subject.

11. Title Tittle-Tattle

The library media specialist makes index cards that resemble the following: "I am thinking of a specific fiction book. It's a classic teenage contemporary story. It's about a boy called Chris Boyd. The book begins: 'I'm just going to tell you the story the way it happened, and I'm afraid it's going to shock a few people. Most of what I'm going to confess has to do with when I was fifteen years old. But I'm sixteen now, so I'm not as demented as I was then.' Chris is a shabby, raggy, depressed kid who hates his mother and live-in nurse, and aches for the day when he will be able to wear his deceased father's chesterfield coat. Chris is stuck in a house with a dying lady and her thirty-year-old eccentric son, Lloyd Dipardi. He teaches Chris about life." Students may decide the name of the book.

12. Fiction Finagle

Once again, the class is divided into two teams, A and B. The library media specialist gives both teams a list of ten fiction titles. The teams must substitute a rhyming syllable for a portion of the title. For example, a member from team A will say out loud to team B, "Tanwolf." Team B must guess the correct title: *Manwolf* (Skurzynski). The team who guesses the most correct titles in a specified time is the winner.

1. *Manwolf* (Skurzynski). (can-, stand-, tan-, ban-, land-, sand-, dan-wolf.)
2. *Watership Down* (Adams). (water-lip, -skip, -tip, town, hound, bound.)
3. *Jaws* (Benchley). (laws.)
4. *Kim* (Kipling). (limb, Tim, gym.)
5. *Blaze* (Somerlott). (haze, daze, craze.)
6. *Deenie* (Blume). (beanie, genie.)

7. *Treasure Island* (Stevenson). (measure, pleasure island.)
8. *Call of the Wild* (London). (call of the mild, tiled, styled.)
9. *Pigman* (Zindel). (jig-, dig-; -band, -sand, -land.)
10. *Red Pawns* (Wibberly). (red lawns, fawns.)
11. *Tiger Eyes* (Blume). (tiger dyes, buys, lies.)
12. *Carrie* (King). (Mary, Larry, scary.)
13. *High King* (Alexander). (bye, sky; sing, zing.)
14. *Jungle Book* (Kipling). (jungle; look, cook, nook.)
15. *Silmarillion* (Tolkien). (mill, kill, till; where, care, bear; bill, ill; con, John, wand.)
16. *Witches of Worm* (Snyder). (witches of germ, firm.)
17. *Sign of the Owl* (Chester). (line, kind, find; fowl, jowl, cowl.)
18. *Creep* (Dodson). (leap, jeep, beep.)
19. Icarus Seal (Hyde). (Icarus teal, meal, steal.)
20. Walls (Daly). (halls, calls, malls.)

13. Travel Agency Alphabet

Group the class into two teams. Each member of the team must contribute the name of a city or town. The first person of Team A gives a city beginning with the letter A; the first person of Team B names a city beginning with the letter B, and so on, until ending with the letter Z. The team with the most cities is the winner. If a member of the team is unable to come up with any city or town, the opposing team may have a try. If they are also unable to think of a city, the original team may have one more try at it. If they cannot come up with an answer, it may go back to the opposing team once more. If, with the second try, they are still unable to name a city, the letter is thrown out.

14. Personality Potpourri

Each student chooses to become a famous personality. The first student chooses a famous person — for instance, John Kennedy. He gives a clue, "the letter K," to the others. Students, in turn, must ask a question to find out who "K" is. The first student may ask: "Are

you a scientist?" He would answer, "No." The second student may
ask: "Are you a president of the United States?" He would say, "Yes."
The third student may ask: "Were you assassinated while in office?"
The answer would be, "Yes." This continues until students guess the
personality.

15. Back-To-Back

Here once again is an activity that may be correlated to any
of the subjects in the curriculum, or it may be used solely as a library-
oriented game. The topic is chosen, whether it be fiction titles; author
names; famous book characters; biographies; science vocabulary
terms; etc.

If fiction titles are used, the library media specialist begins by
giving a title, for instance, *Freckle Juice* by Judy Blume. Each student
then, in turn, must give a fiction title beginning with the last letter
of the title previously given (disregarding articles such as "the"). 1.
Freckle Juice. 2. *Escape to Witch Mountain.* 3. *The Night Before
Christmas.* 4. *The Shining.* 5. *The Genessee Queen.* 6. *Notes for
Another Life.* 7. *Effect of Gamma Rays on Man-in-the-Moon
Marigolds.* 8. *Starring Sally J. Freedman As Herself.* 9. *Firestarter.*
10. *Rumble Fish.* 11. *High King.* 12. *Green Hills of Africa.* This activity may be used as a game with the class divided into two groups
or used with the class as a whole going around once or twice.

16. Spooks

Split the class into groups of 4 or 5 students. Student 1 calls out
a letter, perhaps an "L." Student 2 calls out another letter, maybe an
"I," being careful not to form a complete word. (Note, however, that
the letters called out must have the *potential* for forming a word —
that is, Student 2 could not call out "X" or "Q.") Student 3 continues
the process of adding a letter without completing the word. (At this
point, students should be trying to force others to complete the word;
for example, Student 3 might add a "V," trying to force Student 4 to
add an "E" to complete the word LIVE. However, Student 4 could
thwart this plan by adding an "I," forcing some other student to complete a word—perhaps LIVID or LIVING.) The student who com-

pletes the word becomes a "Spook" and is out of the game. This keeps
up until only one student remains un"spooked."

17. Solid-Liquid-Gas

This game may be employed in any subject area. Specifically
applied to the sciences, the categories applied may be animal,
vegetable, or mineral; or solid, liquid, or gas. One student thinks of
something in one category: for instance, hydrogen. He says, "I am
thinking of a gas." Other students may have up to twenty questions
to decide what the object or matter is. Break the class into two teams.

18. Teacher

A list of topics studied in a particular classroom during the
marking period is given to the librarian. These topics are put on individual index cards or pieces of paper, and put into a box. Upon
visiting the library, each member of the class picks one card out of the
box, and must speak without hesitation about the topic, even if it is
nonsense. Whoever speaks the most intelligently for thirty seconds is
the winner. If there are a number of winners, these students draw
another topic from the box, and must speak for one minute, the winner being the student who survives the longest, with the most in-
telligent speech.

19. Scavenger Hunt

The class is divided into two teams. Each team gets a set of ten
directions. For example, (1) Find a fiction book with the author's
name beginning with S, and the title beginning with T; (2) Find a
nonfiction book about computers; (3) What is the meaning of
"tolbutamide"? What source does this answer come from? What is the
page number? (4) How many books can you find in your library written by Robert Heinlein? (5) How many books can you find in your
library written by Irene Hunt? (6) What was the "Bland-Allison Act"?
(Source and page.) (7) What topic is represented by 629.22? (8) What
are three books written by Paul Zindel? (9) Who was Felix Dahn?
(Source and page.) (10) Name five short stories by Edgar Allan Poe.
The team who finishes the scavenger hunt first is the winner.

20. What's My Name?

The social studies or English class may find this activity a pleasant diversion on a visit to the library media center. One student has a name of a famous person pinned on his/her back. Other students, in turn, give him or her a clue as to who this person is. The student who is pinned must find out who he or she is in the least number of guesses possible.

21. Mixer

Each class member is given a folded piece of paper with information written on it, or students may draw these from a box. Each piece of paper matches up with another; for instance, a call number on one piece matches with a topic on another. Other possibilities are a title of a book, an author; a question, an answer; etc. Each piece of paper should have only one bit of information, that is, only the book title, or only a call number.

Students then group themselves in pairs, matching themselves to each other.

22. Recognition

I have used this game as a contest. Students must guess the title of a fiction book which these objects, animals, places or people suggest:

1. an unexpected party. (*The Hobbit*, Tolkien.)
2. rabbits. (*Watership Down*, Adams.)
3. Lilliputians, people somewhat under 6". (*Gulliver's Travels*, Swift.)
4. a hot air balloon. (*Around the World in Eighty Days*, Verne.)
5. freckles. (*Freckle Juice*, Blume.)
6. a leather mask. (*Manwolf*, Skurzynski.)
7. Tiny Tim. (*A Christmas Carol*, Dickens.)
8. the watcher. (*A Watcher in the Woods*, Randall.)

9. a lighthouse in space. (*The Keeper of the Isis Light*, Hughes.)
10. a white whale. (*Moby Dick*, Melville.)
11. a tesseract. (*A Wrinkle in Time*, L'Engle.)
12. Mr. Pignati. (*The Pigman*, Zindel.)
13. Ramad of the wolves. (*Caves of Fire and Ice*, Murphy.)
14. a cat named Worm. (*The Witches of Worm*, Snyder.)
15. The sea chest. (*Treasure Island*, Stevenson.)
16. Maple Hill. (*Miracles on Maple Hill*, Sorensen.)
17. a cabin. (*Uncle Tom's Cabin*, Stowe.)
18. Spidermonkey Island. (*The Voyages of Doctor Doolittle*, Lofting.)
19. harmonica music. (*Escape to Witch Mountain*, Key.)
20. a burned right hand. (*Johnny Tremain*, Forbes.)
21. a blue willow plate. (*Blue Willow*, Gates.)
22. the Nautilus. (*Twenty Thousand Leagues Under the Sea*, Verne.)
23. Carlsbad Caverns. (*Secret of the Bats*, Stewart.)
24. a sorrel colt. (*The Red Pony*, Steinbeck.)
25. a lovable English schoolmaster. (*Goodbye, Mr. Chips*, Hilton.)

23. Magazine Madness

Here is another activity I have used as a monthly contest. Students must decide what magazine is suggested by the following (all of the magazines are found in our library so that they may browse at the magazine rack):

1. Sixteen plus one? (*Seventeen.*)
2. Epoch? (*Time.*)
3. Productive calculating? (*Creative Computing.*)
4. All? (*Omni.*)
5. Drawings and projects? (*Arts and Activities.*)
6. Well-liked operation? (*Popular Mechanics.*)
7. Games pictured? (*Sports Illustrated.*)
8. Well-liked knowledge? (*Popular Science.*)

9. Knowledge condensed? (*Science Digest.*)
10. Residence workings? (*Home Mechanix.*)
11. A country's land? (*National Geographic.*)
12. A male child's existence? (*Boys' Life.*)
13. A snow sport? (*Skiing.*)
14. Peruser's abstract? (*Reader's Digest.*)
15. Engine tendency? (*Motor Trend.*)
16. A summer sport shortened? (*Baseball Digest.*)
17. Outside existence? (*Outdoor Life.*)
18. Labor and seat? (*Workbench.*)
19. Academy drawings? (*School Arts.*)
20. A fall sport condensed? (*Football Digest.*)
21. Information for seven days? (*Newsweek.*)
22. Adolescent? (*Teen.*)
23. Fast car? (*Hot Rod.*)
24. A famous museum? (*Smithsonian.*)
25. A dynamo bike? (*Motorcyclist.*)
26. Buyer's disclosure and purchasing model? (*Consumer Report & Buying Guide.*)
27. Academy and room of books and notebook? (*School Library Journal.*)
28. A country's land globe? (*National Geographic World.*)
29. Relatives estimating? (*Family Computing.*)
30. American bulletins and the earth's story? (*U.S. News & World Report.*)
31. Volume file? (*Booklist.*)

24. Title Search

Box or circle as many fiction titles as you can find (there are 51 in this story):

It's like this, cat: Uncle Tom's cabin is the house without a Christmas tree. But at least they sang a Christmas carol on the night before Christmas. How would you like to go around the world in eighty days? Annie and Christine, the little women on Main Street, together with Johnny Tremain, left for a visit to William Blake's Inn by the shores of Silver Lake. They stayed at a castle. Jennifer, Hecate, Macbeth, William McKinley, and me, Elizabeth also went by way of twenty-one balloons. We crossed the *bridge to Terabithia* and the *island of the blue dolphins. 1984* has *gone with the wind*; it was *a long winter* and it has been *all quiet on the western front. Mrs. Frisby and the rats of NIMH,* staying in a *little town on the prairie,* ran into *millions of cats* and *the witch of blackbird pond. That was then, this is now. I never loved your mind, Mrs. Mike. I love you, stupid old yeller. Then again, maybe I won't, big red. Across five Aprils, tiger eyes* and *rumble fish* and *the blind colt* became ill, but with aid of *the pistachio prescription* they were fine *forever. Tom Sawyer* turned *fifteen* Saturday and won *a red badge of courage. The pigman kidnapped the outsiders* plus *Cujo.* He found *the shining black pearl* next to *the diary of Anne Frank* where *the firestarter* worked the *night shift.*

25. Famous First Lines

Students guess the titles of well-known fiction books from which these first lines come:

1. "Call me Ishmael." (*Moby Dick*, Melville.)
2. "I don't think I'll ever get married." (*It's Not the End of the World*, Blume.)
3. "Late in the afternoon of a chilly day in February, two gentlemen were sitting alone over their wine in a well-furnished dining-parlor, in the town of P____, in Kentucky." (*Uncle Tom's Cabin*, Stowe.)
4. "Mr. Phileas Fogg lived, in 1872, at No. 7, Saville Row, Burlington Gardens, the house in which Sheridan died in 1814." (*Around the World in Eighty Days*, Verne.)
5. "Like silent, hungry sharks that swim in the darkness of the sea, the German submarines arrived in the middle of the night." (*The Cay*, Taylor.)
6. "In a hole in the ground there lived a hobbit." (*The Hobbit*, Tolkien.)
7. "Marley was dead, to begin with." (*A Christmas Carol*, Dickens.)
8. "Miyax pushed back the hood of her sealskin parka and looked at the Arctic sun." (*Julie of the Wolves*, George.)

9. "The worst winter in fifty years, the old Scotsman had told me. I'd only been around for sixteen, but it was the worst I'd seen, and I was willing to take his word for the other thirty-four." (*Mrs. Mike*, Freedman.)

10. "It was a wild, windy, southwestern spring when the idea of killing Mr. Griffin occurred to them." (*Killing Mr. Griffin*, Duncan.)

11. "There are dragons in the twins' vegetable garden." (*A Wind in the Door*, L'Engle.)

12. "I first met Jennifer on my way to school. It was Halloween, and she was sitting in a tree." (*Jennifer, Hecate, Macbeth, William McKinley, and Me, Elizabeth*, Konigsburg.)

13. "Once there were three patients who met in the hospital and decided to live together. They arrived at this decision because they had no place to go when they were discharged." (*Tell Me That You Love Me, Junie Moon*, Kellogg.)

14. "Squire Trelawney, Dr. Livesey, and the rest of these gentlemen having asked me to write down the whole particulars about Treasure Island, from the beginning to the end, keeping nothing back but the bearings of the island, and that only because there is still treasure not yet lifted, I take up my pen in the year of grace 17__, and go back to the time when my father kept the 'Admiral Benbow' Inn, and the brown old seaman, with the sabre cut, first took up his lodging under our roof." (*Treasure Island*, Stevenson.)

15. "My father is always talking about how a dog can be very educational for a boy. This is one reason I got a cat." (*It's Like This Cat*, Neville.)

16. "A long time ago, when all the grandfathers and grandmothers of today were little boys and little girls or very small babies, or perhaps not even born, Pa and Ma and Mary and Laura and Baby Carrie left their little house in the big woods of Wisconsin." (*Little House on the Prairie*, Wilder.)

17. "My mother named me Deenie because right before I was born she saw a movie about a beautiful girl named Wilmadeene, who everybody called Deenie for short." (*Deenie*, Blume.)

18. "There are two kinds of travel. The usual way is to take the fastest imaginable conveyance along the shortest road. The other way is not to care particularly where you are going or how long it will take you, or whether you will get there or not." (*The Twenty-One Balloons*, Du Bois.)

26. Famous Last Lines

Played like Famous First Lines, above, using final lines of novels.

27. Decode the Title

Decode the following fiction book titles.

1. A TWECHAR NI HET SOWOD. (*A Watcher in the Woods*, Randall.)
2. KERLEFC CUJIE. (*Freckle Juice*, Blume.)
3. WAMONFL. (*Manwolf*, Skurzynski.)
4. A LEWINRK NI MITE. (*A Wrinkle in Time*, L'Engle.)
5. HET BIHOBT. (*The Hobbit*, Tolkien.)
6. CIHWT FO LCARIBDKB DONP. (*Witch of Blackbird Pond*, Speare.)
7. RICAER. (*Carrie*, King.)
8. LASNID FO TEH LUEB LIDNOPSH. (*Island of the Blue Dolphins*, O'Dell.)
9. RUCADAL. (*Dracula*, Stoker.)
10. YM RIADNGL YM BUHEMGARR. (*My Darling, My Hamburger*, Zindel.)
11. YMOB KIDC. (*Moby Dick*, Melville.)
12. HTE LACL OF HET LWID. (*The Call of the Wild*, London.)
13. NECUL MO'TS BANIC. (*Uncle Tom's Cabin*, Stowe.)
14. 8941. (*1984*, Orwell.)
15. ETH YAC. (*The Cay*, Taylor.)
16. A HRSASTCIM RAOLC. (*A Christmas Carol*, Dickens.)

17. RARETEUS NISADL. (*Treasure Island*, Stevenson.)
18. NUGEJL KOOB. (*Jungle Book*, Kipling.)
19. DER NOPY. (*Red Pony*, Steinbeck.)
20. BELBURB. (*Blubber*, Blume.)
21. DER DEBAG FO ROGUCEA. (*Red Badge of Courage*, Crane.)
22. DETAERSUVN FO CEHRUYBEKRL NIFN. (*Adventures of Huckleberry Finn*, Twain.)
23. TEFIEFN. (*Fifteen*, Cleary.)
24. VEIL DUNRE HET NSU. (*Evil Under the Sun*, Christie.)
25. WAJS. (*Jaws*, Benchley.)

28. Synonymy

This is a good activity for English or reading classes. The aim is to find a synonym (word with a similar meaning) for each word on a list. If the student can think of more than one synonym, he should write the shortest one he can think of. After ten or fifteen minutes, the list is checked by the teacher and the library media specialist. The winner is the student who finds a synonym for the most words. If more than one student has an equal number of synonyms, the winner is the student who has the least amount of letters in his synonyms.

29. Pastiche

Students are given a word or words, of say, seven to fifteen letters, such as *romance*. Each letter must be used as the initial letter of a title of a romance book. Or use any other genre of fiction. The first title must begin with an R, the second with an O, etc., until all the letters have titles written next to them. The winner is the student who first completes the activity.

R — *Red Room* (Dobkin)
O — *One on One* (Ketter)
M — *My Lucky Star* (Cassiday)
A — *April Love Story* (Cooney)
N — *New Beginning* (Ryan)
C — *Call Me Beautiful* (Blair)
E — *Exchange of Hearts* (Quin-Harkin)

30. Famous Quotations

1. "A whale ship was my Yale College and my Harvard." (Herman Melville.)

2. "If winter comes, can spring be far behind?" (Percy Bysshe Shelley.)

3. "Neither a borrower nor a lender be." (William Shakespeare.)

4. "In winter I get up at night and dress by yellow candlelight." (Robert Louis Stevenson.)

5. "The best is yet to be." (Robert Browning.)

6. "Ask me no questions, and I'll tell you no lies." (Oliver Goldsmith.)

7. "I wants to make your flesh creep." (Charles Dickens.)

8. "My candle burns at both ends." (Edna St. Vincent Millay.)

9. "Sweets to the sweet." (William Shakespeare.)

10. "Truth is stranger than fiction." (George Gordon, Lord Byron.)

11. "When lilacs last in the door-yard bloomed." (Walt Whitman.)

12. "By hook or by crook." (John Wycliffe.)

13. "For in the stars is written the death of every man." (Geoffrey Chaucer.)

14. "Happy is the house that shelters a friend!" (Ralph Waldo Emerson.)

15. "Knowledge is power." (Francis Bacon.)

16. "Eureka!" (Archimedes.)

17. "Don't give up the ship." (Commander James Lawrence, USN.)

18. "A chip off the old block." (Edmund Burke.)

19. "Give me liberty, or give me death!" (Patrick Henry.)

20. "Know thyself." (Plutarch.)

21. "Let them eat cake." (Jean Jacques Rousseau.)

22. "A penny for your thoughts." (John Heywood.)

23. "Speak softly and carry a big stick." (Theodore Roosevelt.)

24. "Quoth the raven, Nevermore." (Edgar Allan Poe.)

25. "Nothing is so much to be feared as fear." (Henry David Thoreau.)

31. Well-Known Excerpts

A variation on Famous Quotations, above, using famous fiction titles. Select 10–20 well-known novels. Choose a line or short paragraph from each book. Make dittos of these to pass out to the group. Students must guess from which book the quotes were taken. The student who guesses the most is the winner.

32. Rebus

Students love guessing the titles of famous fiction books, "spelled" out as rebuses. I design these titles by cutting pictures out of discarded magazines and putting them on construction paper. The pictures plus an occasional word or letter represent the title. Some of these may be quite challenging.

33. Mystery Question

Another one of our monthly contests is mystery question. Whoever first answers the secret mystery question correctly wins first prize. Examples of questions:

1. Who wrote *Warrior Scarlet*? (Rosemary Sutcliff. Answer found in card catalog.)
2. Who was George Inness? (American landscape painter, 1825–1894. *Webster's Biographical Dictionary*.)
3. Who invented the first player piano? (John McTammany, Jr., on June 14, 1881. *Famous First Facts*.)
4. What is a synonym for the word "humbug"? (Nonsense. *The Doubleday Roget's Thesaurus in Dictionary Form*.)
5. What and where is Leidy Peak? (Mountain, 12,015 ft., in North Unintah Co., eastern Utah. *Webster's Geographical Dictionary*.)
6. What is "Least Squares"? (A method of fitting an equation to a set of data, the resulting equation being

considered the best-fitting equation. *The Harper Encyclopedia of Science.*)

7. What book did Kate Seredy write whose title begins with the word "the"? (*The Good Master.* Card catalog.)

8. What was the original meaning of the word "cobalt"? (A devil. *Word Origins and Their Romantic Stories.*)

9. In sports, what is the meter rule? (A rule regulating the building of certain classes of sailboats by requiring the overall dimensions to conform to a specific formula. *Webster's Sports Dictionary.*)

10. What is the copyright date of the book *Adam of the Road* by Gray? (1942. Card catalog.)

11. What was the population of Albuquerque, New Mexico, in 1980? (24,024. *The World Almanac and Book of Facts.*)

12. What are the colors of the Belgian flag? (Black, yellow, red. *The World Almanac and Book of Facts.*)

13. From what country did the composer Alexander Borodin come? (Russia. *Great Composers 1300–1900.*)

14. When was the National League of Women Voters founded? (1920. *Dictionary of American History.*)

15. What is Boniface? (It is the name of eight popes of the Roman Catholic Church. *The World Book Encyclopedia.*)

16. Where is the spleen located? (Behind the left lower ribs and extending behind the stomach and midriff. *Fishbein's Illustrated Medical and Health Encyclopedia.*)

17. Who wrote the quotation, "In winter I get up at night and dress by yellow candle-light"? (Robert Louis Stevenson. *Magill's Quotations in Context.*)

18. Who wrote the book *Rabble on a Hill*? (Robert Altar. Card catalog.)

19. In Indian mythology, what does Surya stand for? (The sun. *Larousse Encyclopedia of Mythology.*)

20. Who wrote the book *A Wrinkle in Time*? (Madeleine L'Engle. Card catalog.)

34. Egghead

An art exhibit is arranged. Various slides are produced from famous paintings, or the library media specialist holds up a good reference book of various reproductions. The class is divided into two teams. The teams are supplied with a list of famous painters and their paintings. The team who correctly matches the most titles and artists to the paintings shown is the winner, with the loser being the egghead.

35. Composite Issues

The English class may participate in this activity. The class is divided into four teams. Two groups of index cards with printed topics on them are put into two separate boxes. The boxes are passed to each group, each team selecting one card from each box. The teams are instructed to create a one-page composition using these two topics. The composition must make some sense: one topic should flow into the next topic.

After a set time limit, say twenty minutes, the teams read their compositions. The teams are given a score from 1–10 with 10 as the highest score. The English teacher and the library media specialist may judge the winner.

36. Newsweek

National Affairs	International News	The Arts
Society	Business	Lifestyle
Potpourri	Political Campaigns	State News

This activity could be used with the social studies group to acquaint them with current events and prominent people in the news. On a chalkboard, write topics such as the above. You may add another row of topics to make it larger.

The group is divided into two teams, A and B. Each team will have a captain chosen by flipping a coin, calling "heads" or "tails." The team selects a category, and the teacher or librarian asks questions from a list prepared by the librarian. The team captain is the spokesman and gives the answer once the team confers. The librarian writes an A on the chalkboard next to the category if Team A answers correctly; or a B next to the category if Team B answers correctly. Each team tries to get three in a row, and that team is the winner; or, whichever team gets the most answers correct is the winner.

37. Strange Lingo

The foreign language class may enjoy this activity with the help of a foreign language dictionary and instructor. We employ, for example, *The Concise Dictionary of Twenty-Six Languages in Simultaneous Translations* compiled by Peter M. Bergman. Students enjoy seeing and hearing words in numerous tongues.

Make up 5 × 7 index cards or 8 × 11 sheets of typewriter paper as follows: Print a word on each card or sheet in a specific language, and on the back write the language. For instance, OUI (back of card: French). On other cards: SÍ (Spanish); SÌ (Italian); SIM (Portuguese); DA (Rumanian); JA (German); JA (Swedish); TAK (Polish); DA (Russian); NE (Greek); HAI (Japanese); etc. Use as few or as many languages as you like. Select ten to fifteen words. After going through all the words, select cards at random, and see who can guess what the meaning and language is. Divide the group into two teams, and score one point if they get the meaning correct, and one point if they get the language correct. The winner is the team that gets the highest score.

38. French Relay

Students must follow directions in French for this game. The group is once again divided into two teams. With the cooperation of the foreign language teacher, ten instructions are written down on paper. Students must complete the ten instructions. Whichever team first completes all ten instructions completely and correctly is the winner. Other languages may be used, of course.

39. U.S. Open

Once again the class is divided into two to four teams. Students are given 18 algebraic equations on a ditto sheet. On the bulletin board is a diagram of an 18-hole golf course. Each team must complete the algebraic equation correctly in order to go onto the next hole. (Use a one-minute time limit.) The answer is sealed under the hole with masking tape. The librarian peels the tape away after answers are given to check for accuracy. The team who completes the 18-hole course correctly is the winner.

40. Mathematical Candyland

This is a fun activity for the math class. Use Milton Bradley's "Candyland" boards or make a game board with colored squares of posterboard if you cannot procure the original boards. Choose various colors for the different levels of difficulty. For example, pink for arithmetic problems; red for word problems; blue for algebraic problems; green for geometric problems. Make up 20–25 cards with a problem on each one; at the bottom of each card, mark squares of the appropriate color.

Students are divided into five groups with no more than four to a group. Each member of the group takes the top card from the pile, and must give an answer within one minute. If he fails, he may not advance; if he answers correctly, he may advance as many squares as are marked on the card. For instance, if there are two red squares on the card, he may advance two red squares on the board, if he answers correctly. The winner of each group is the student who reaches the end of the candyland path.

41. Doubles

This activity may be played by grouping the class into fours: two students playing against two students. Each pair is given a stack of index cards with questions and answers on them. The serving team, Team A, poses a question to the opposing team, Team B. If they fail to answer correctly, then Team A receives a point (called 15, as in tennis scoring). If Team B answers correctly, then they receive the point (called 15). This continues until one team scores 4 points, and leads by at least 2 points. (The first point is called 15; the second is 30; the third is 40; and the fourth is called game point; a score of zero is called love.)

The server's score is given first. If both teams win 3 points, or 40, it is called deuce. If you wish to take doubles past winning the game, the first team to win two sets wins the Doubles Tennis Match.

42. Illustrious Names

Choose a letter of the alphabet, and name all the historical figures that come to mind whose names begin with that letter. You may include fiction book authors, prominent people in the news, fiction characters, etc. Divide the group into two teams. The team that comes up with the most names is the winner.

43. Roulette

A roulette wheel is made out of oak tag (or use an existing board from another game). The categorical divisions of the wheel are genres of fiction: science fiction, classics, historical fiction, contemporary classics, etc. Each member of the English class may spin the spinner. Each student selects a book of that genre to read and later to report on briefly. Upon returning to the library, the class members may give 1–3 characteristics of the genre, and apply them to their particular book. (For example, historical fiction deals with a factual setting even though the story is not something that really happened.)

44. Character Climb

An oak tag or construction paper board is made with rungs of a ladder. Split the group into two teams, Team 1 and 2. Questions concerning the library, fiction books, and nonfiction books are alternately asked of each team. If the team answers correctly, move a construction paper marker with tape up one rung; if incorrect, move down one rung. The winning team is the first team to reach the top of the ladder.

45. Around the World in 80 Days

The class is separated into two teams, A and B. Each member of the team will "travel" to a different town or city of the world. Each person is given an index card with the name of a city or town on it (and the country in parentheses). Team A begins, with the first team member reading the city. Team B has 4 chances to guess the correct country in which the city is located. If they can do it in four guesses, they receive 5 points; if not, they get a minus 5. The team with the highest score wins.

46. Fantasia

This activity once again may be employed by dividing the class into two teams. The library media specialist reads, from prepared index cards, the descriptions of settings from a number of fantasy books. The group must decide from which fantasy title each description was taken.

47. Whimsical Sallies

Each member of the class reads a humorous fiction book. Each must present to the group a 30-second to 1-minute presentation of a funny incident that took place in this book. No one is permitted to laugh or even crack a smile.

48. Classical Gas

The class is divided into two teams. Each team faces the opposing team. The game is played like Cross Questions (see *Back to Books*): The teacher or library media specialist asks questions of each student, alternating teams. In this version, however, the questions should be about classic books. Credit is given for knowing a title and/or an author—one point per correct answer. The team with the highest score wins.

49. Lotto

Tickets are sold for 10–25¢ apiece. Each ticket has a number on it. Tickets are placed in a box, and mixed up. At the end of an allotted time, say 1–2 weeks, the library media specialist draws the winning ticket, and it is announced over the school radio station. A prize is won, such as a popular book.

50. Racetrack

This activity may be a contest between English classes. It may also be revised to correlate with other subject classes. Each English class is assigned a number at the starting gate. The winning class is the first to complete the race course by completing the assignment at each gate.

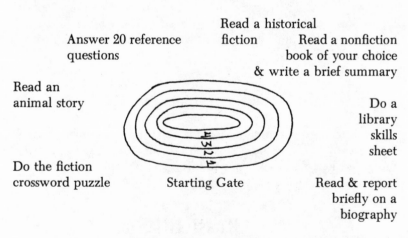

Answer 20 reference questions

Read a historical fiction

Read a nonfiction book of your choice & write a brief summary

Read an animal story

Do a library skills sheet

Do the fiction crossword puzzle

Starting Gate

Read & report briefly on a biography

51. Football

Same as Racetrack. Each team aims toward the goal post. The winning team is the one who gets to the goal first. Starting at the 50-yard line, each team competes to get to the opposite goal line. Each yard line represents a specific assignment or question to answer correctly. If the activity is used like cross questions, a wrong answer will put the team back a yard line, and a right response will advance the team a yard line.

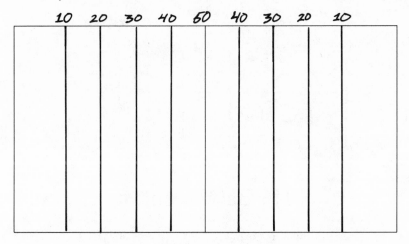

52. Weight Lifting

Once again, this activity may be geared for any subject. Each weight designates a specific task to be completed. This may include: a book read; research questions answered; etc. Two classes may compete, with the winner being the class who can "lift the heaviest weights," or correctly complete the assignments.

WEIGHTS	WEIGHTS
10 lbs	10 lbs
20 lbs	20 lbs
50 lbs	50 lbs
100 lbs	100 lbs
250 lbs	250 lbs
500 lbs	500 lbs

53. Steeplechase

Same as Racetrack. This game is comprised of 28 "hurdles" and "water jumps" (see figure below).

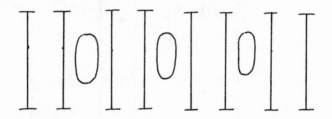

54. Baby Contest

Faculty members bring in baby pictures of themselves. These are displayed in the library, with each picture numbered. Students must decide which photograph belongs to which teacher. The student who guesses the most wins a prize.

55. Literary Labors

One of our seventh grade English teachers guides a couple of the classes to produce "books." Each student writes a "book," illustrates it, and covers it. These "books" are displayed in the library for a good portion of the school year. Students enjoy reading the creations of their fellows.

56. Yachting

Two social studies classes may participate in this activity, or one class may be divided into two teams. The winner is the team that guesses the most correct answers. The library media specialist names a river, and students must guess where this river outflows, that is, the ocean into which the river flows:

1. Amazon. (Atlantic.)
2. Columbia. (Pacific.)
3. Weser. (North Sea.)
4. Nile. (Mediterranean.)
5. Zambezi. (Indian Ocean.)
6. Danube. (Black Sea.)
7. Rio Grande. (Gulf of Mexico.)
8. Indus. (Arabian Sea.)
9. Rhine. (North Sea.)
10. Seine. (English Channel.)
11. Po. (Adriatic Sea.)
12. Oder. (Baltic Sea.)

57. Skiing

Same as Yachting. Students must name the country or the continent in which the following mountains are found:

1. McKinley. (U.S. — Alaska.)
2. Whitney. (U.S. — California.)
3. Bear. (U.S. — Alaska.)
4. Colima. (Mexico.)
5. Mont Blanc. (Europe — French Alps.)
6. Mana. (India.)
7. Andrew Jackson. (Antarctica.)
8. Broad. (Kashmir.)
9. Montcalm. (Spain.)
10. Toubkal. (Morocco.)
11. MacKellar. (Antarctica.)
12. Ras Dashan. (Ethiopia.)
13. Yale. (U.S. — Colorado.)
14. Ranier. (U.S. — Washington State.)
15. Pular. (Chile.)
16. Amne Machin. (China.)
17. Kinabalu. (Malaysia.)
18. Zupo. (Switzerland.)
19. Api. (Nepal.)
20. Mandala. (New Guinea.)
21. Kilimanjaro. (Tanzania.)
22. Cook. (New Zealand.)

23. Chamlang. (Nepal.)
24. Elger. (Switzerland.)
25. Kazbek. (U.S.S.R.)

58. Volleyball

The class is divided into Teams A and B. The bulletin board sketched below can be used to follow the action of this game, with a paper "ball" being moved back and forth. The library media specialist prepares a list of questions concerning the library and books. The specialist then addresses a question to a person on Team A. If that person answers correctly, Team A wins a point, and the next question is addressed to the next person on Team A. This continues until Team A answers incorrectly. The "ball" (question) then goes to Team B. However, as in real volleyball, Team B does not win a point for a correct answer in this case, because Team A was the "serving" team. A correct answer wins the serve for Team B, and questions are then posed to members of that team, with points won for correct answers. When a question is missed, the serve returns to Team A. No student may answer two questions in a row. Students try to slam the ball into the opposite court by giving the correct answer, and thus gaining one point. The opposing team gains a point if a team talks or tries to help a team member. Each individual team member must answer the question on his own. The first team to score 15 points wins the game, but they must win by a two-point margin.

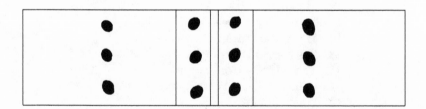

59. Billiards

Two teams are formed once again. Correctly answering questions regarding the library or books pockets the ball. There are 15 "balls," or questions. Players score one point each time a question is correctly answered. Answering 8 of the 15 questions correctly, that is, pocketing 8 of the 15 balls, wins the game for the team. A bulletin board display such as the one below may be used to act out the game; construction paper balls are pocketed as questions are answered.

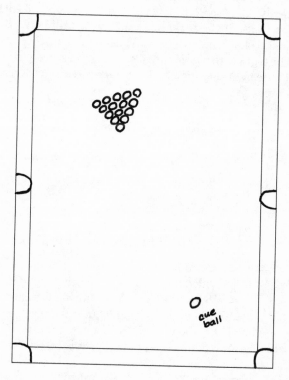

60. Major League Baseball

Two teams are formed. The manager of the teams, the library media specialist, makes up a list of questions for the teams' lineup and "batting" order. Each member of the team at bat is asked one question. If three members of the team answer incorrectly—"strike out"—the opposing team is then up at bat. A turn at bat for both teams comprises an inning. The team with the most "runs" or correct answers at the end of an inning wins. Or play more than one inning if there is time.

61. Intramural Bowling

The class is divided into two teams. Each pin represents a question. Upon answering a question correctly, one pin is knocked down. Team A is asked 10 consecutive questions. If the team answers all 10 correctly, they score a strike. Then Team B is asked 10 consecutive questions. If the team does not answer all correctly, their score is equal to the number of pins knocked down, that is, correct answers. The team with the most strikes or highest score is the winner. You can act the game out on a bulletin board, with pins arranged as shown below.

62. Fiction Roll

The group is divided into two teams. Each team must give the name of an adventure book, etc. Students may use the card catalog, or titles may come from their heads. Whichever team comes up with the completed list first is the winner. In the case of a tie, whichever team provides the most fiction titles wins. Possible categories to use include: (1) adventure; (2) animal; (3) fantasy; (4) historical fiction; (5) supernatural; (6) mystery; (7) Newbery Award winners; (8) romance; (9) science fiction; (10) classics.

63. Letters to Authors

Students are encouraged to write letters to noted fiction authors. Addresses may be provided by the library media specialist. English classes may like to participate in composing a letter from the class inquiring how the author got started writing, how he/she gets ideas for writing, etc.

64. Jigsaw Puzzles

Book jackets of fiction books are photocopied, and then cut into pieces of a jigsaw puzzle. The English class is divided into two teams, Team A and B. The library media specialist tacks or tapes one piece of the puzzle to the bulletin board, and students try to guess the title of the book. Team A guesses first. If incorrect, one additional piece is tacked onto the board, and Team B has one guess. The team that guesses the title wins 5 points. The team with the most points is the winner.

65. Round-Robin

Each English class comes to the library for one class period or perhaps half the period. A list of questions pertaining to the library or to fiction books will have been prepared by the library media specialist, who will ask each member of the class a question from the list. If the pupil correctly answers the question, a point is given. If the student does not answer the question correctly, the next student is asked. If that student also does not answer correctly, the third student is asked. If this student fails to answer the question correctly, the question is thrown out. This continues until a set number of questions — for example, 50 — have been asked.

The English class with the highest score wins the Round-Robin series. This activity may be used for any of the subjects in the curriculum.

66. License

This idea corresponds to any of the classes. A license is a questionnaire that must be completed correctly before the student is awarded it. For instance, students may receive a license for: chef; electrician; pilot; animal trainer; accountant; etc. Students must research these questions in the library, and fill in the appropriate answers to be awarded the license.

67. Diploma

Upon completing a specific task, students may be awarded a "diploma." Students must write a very brief summary to show to their English teacher or to the library media specialist, indicating that the task was completed.

Diploma	*Task to be completed*
Grammar School	Read 5 short stories — any author.
High School	Read 2 fiction books.
College	Read 5 books — one genre.
Master's Degree	Read 10 books — fiction.
Ph.D.	Read 20 books — fiction — any genre.

68. Horseshoes

Once again, the class is grouped into two teams. Horseshoes are made out of wood or other material. Each student gets 3 horseshoes to throw. In order to receive the 3 horseshoes, however, the student must first answer a question correctly. These questions would apply to library skills or a specific subject of the curriculum. For example, if the science class is visiting the library, questions pertaining to science subject matter would be given. If upon answering the question correctly the team makes at least one ringer with a horseshoe, the team scores a point. Of course, the team with the highest score wins this tournament.

69. Monster Mash

The library media specialist could show a monster movie such as *Dracula* or *Frankenstein* with a video cassette and TV screen. Or present one of the modern supernatural flicks such as Stephen King's *Carrie*.

70. Historical Sketches

This activity is fun for the history class. Upon visiting the library, the class is grouped into two teams. The library media specialist reads short sketches from 5 × 7 index cards. These sketches could be a description of a famous event in history such as a battle of the Revolutionary War, famous acts of Congress, expeditions, etc. These events may be taken from the *Dictionary of American History*.

Members of Team A and Team B alternately must guess the event. If correct, the team wins a point; if incorrect, a point is taken away. The highest score wins the contest.

71. Monthly Crosswords

Design monthly crosswords or puzzles that correspond to the famous birthdays, events, inventions, or anniversaries of the month.

72. Archery

This game may be enlivening to any class. Questions are typed on index cards, and each card is arbitrarily assigned points. Each pupil draws 3 cards from the pack and tries to answer those questions. If he answers correctly, he receives the points assigned. For example, if the 3 questions drawn have a point value of 20, 60, and 100 on the cards, and the student answers correctly, then he is awarded 180 points. The student who gets the highest score wins.

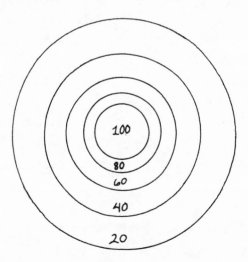

73. Peeping Tom

Display various shoeboxes, gift boxes, or small cardboard boxes. Make little peepholes so that one may look into them. Inside are fiction book covers, along with index cards with a synopsis of the book featured. Change them often.

74. Fictitious Personalities

When the English class drops into the library media center, an enjoyable diversion is Fictitious Personalities. The group sits in a circle, and each is given an index card with a description of a fictional book character written on it. Each is read out loud, and the group tries to guess who the character is. Use any famous character, or narrow it down to a specific genre, although the game is more successful if it includes all types of fictional characters.

Part II

Banquets, Fairs, Parties and Programs

75. Book Fair Fun

Have some fun, and a change of pace. Schedule a book fair in your school library, and watch the enthusiasm of the children. We usually schedule our fair during the month of December, which is a great time of year for purchasing gifts. The Christmas spirit is in the air, and it makes for booming sales. Students are so anxious to buy books that they are continually asking if the library can reserve books until they have enough money to purchase them. They are constantly trying to borrow from each other. We tried out a couple of book fair companies before finding one that fulfilled our needs. Try having one. It's great publicity, and it benefits the library with extra cash.

76. Career Week

Explore possible careers in the math field, or choose other subjects in the curriculum. Invite all of the math classes into the library during this week. With the help of the subject teacher and the guidance department, provide pamphlets, booklets, library books, reference tools, speakers, or any other resource materials. 3×5 or 5×7 index cards could be typed with information on each career, such as salary range, educational requirements, personal characteristics, addresses for further information. Contact people in the field by phone, if possible, and find out a few interesting facts about the job. Ask what they like about their chosen profession, and what they don't like, and relay this information to the students.

77. International Food Day

The library may sponsor an international food day. Various booths or stations may be set up representing different countries: Italy, Germany, China, Poland, U.S.A., Sweden, Greece, etc. Select a handful of recipes from each, and photocopy them for distribution. Each booth displays cookbooks of the country. Select students or library aides to man each booth. Samples of foods may be tasted from each booth. The home economics department may enjoy helping with this project. Some possible countries and foods include: *Italy* — antipasto; pasta; spaghetti. *Germany* — Wienerschnitzel; potato pancakes. *China* — pork fried rice; sweet and sour pork; chicken chow mein. *Holland* — carrot soup. *Hungary* — Hungarian goulash. *France* — marseille fish soup. *Austria* — dumplings. *Belgium & Luxembourg* — fruit tart. *Czechoslovakia* — potato noodles. *Denmark* — Danish pastry; red cabbage. *England, Wales & Northern Ireland* — Yorkshire pudding; beef and kidney pie. *Finland* — cucumber soup. *Norway* — raw potato dumplings. *Poland* — beet soup. *Portugal* — portuguese fish soup.

78. Book Banquet

Another way of having a book fair is to sponsor a book banquet. The idea of this activity is to "sell" books to students. Various booths are set up and decorated with appropriate motifs: seafaring, mystery, contemporary, romance, hobbies, sports, adventure. Student aides may act as salespeople, trying to "sell" their wares. This banquet could last for 2–3 days, allowing the entire school to participate. Each English class may be scheduled into the library at a specific time. The success of this banquet may then be announced as the number of books "sold," or checked out.

79. Vacation Banquet

Hold a travel banquet prior to the February or April vacation week. Feature fiction books with settings in foreign lands; nonfiction books on foreign countries; reference material on other lands; *National Geographic* magazine issues; travel sections from the newspapers. Display travel posters from travel agencies, a globe, and atlases. Have numerous booths sponsoring the various continents: Africa, Asia, Australia, Europe, North America, Central and South America. Make available handouts of interesting facts and trivia about the various countries, points of interest, what it's like to live there, food, climate, etc. Students who check out a book are "travelers."

80. Fall Banquet

Hold a fall banquet during the beginning of the school year, once everyone is oriented, organized, and settled into the environment. Exhibit fiction books on school stories, friendship, sports, as well as nonfiction books on football, soccer, making friends, how to study, how to create a good impression, etc. English classes could visit the library for a 20-minute time slot. Bibliographies should be available on the library's holdings. Type out a few titles on index cards with a synopsis. Decorate the library with back-to-school posters, humorous school signs, and colored leaves.

81. Color Me Beautiful

Arrange for a beautician to visit the library to present a session on beauty and makeup techniques. This could be arranged in cooperation with the home economics department.

82. Live Demonstration

Invite guests to the library media center to demonstrate a skill such as cooking. Invite a chef from a well-known restaurant to prepare a dish or two. Perhaps the home economics department may allow you to use their room. Or invite a musician from the local symphony to perform on an instrument. Or solicit a craftsperson from the town arts and crafts society to illustrate how to make crafts. Or invite an artist to exhibit and illustrate for a short session.

Part III
Bulletin Board Activities

83. On This Day . . .

"On This Day" features a bulletin board or corner of the library recalling a famous invention, anniversary or discovery. Each day recollects some notable event which took place on that particular calendar day in history. For example, if today's date is April 30th, the inscription under the main caption could read: *ON THIS DAY . . . on April 30, 1789, George Washington, the first president of the United States, was inaugurated.* Display biographies of George Washington; reference books on colonial history of the United States; collective biographies of the United States presidents; and interesting trivia about George Washington.

Or, *ON THIS DAY . . . on April 6, 1909, the first polar expedition of which a woman was an associate reached the North Pole.* Exhibit biographies of other woman explorers.

Or, *ON THIS DAY . . . on January 31, 1958, the first satellite to be placed in orbit, the Explorer I, was launched from Cape Canaveral, Fla.* Display newspaper and magazine articles on the progression of the space program from 1958 to the present time.

Or, *ON THIS DAY . . . on January 4, 1885, the first appendectomy, or surgical removal of the appendix, was performed.* Display reference materials and magazine articles on the history of medical progress since 1885.

You may also list a few suggestions for research projects or questions relating to the topic for further investigation. Indicate titles of reference books where information may be found.

84. Judy Blume Day

(Or choose another popular author.) Feature this prolific author on the day or week of her birthday. (Judy Blume's birthday is February 12th, when most schools are out due to Lincoln's birthday.) Students may pick up checklists in order to check off titles read, and they are made aware of novels they would like to read. Have a selection of her works on exhibit (if you can keep them noncirculating long enough!). A poll may be taken for favorite Judy Blume books by having students insert ballots into a box. Cut out book reviews from old issues of *Booklist* and *School Library Journal*. Pin these up on the bulletin board. Photocopy Blume's biography from *Fourth Book of Junior Authors* (de Montreville and Crawford, eds.).

85. Athletic Agility

Photographs of prominent sports figures, stars of the past and present time may be taken from old magazines and newspapers. Choose about 20 sports heroes. Students must recognize who each figure is and the sport played. Representatives from the various sports — baseball, football, soccer, tennis, boxing, etc. — could be chosen.

86. Seasonal Splash

Cut out pictures from old magazines. Have library aides trace and cut out construction paper to back these pictures so that the pictures will stay intact for some time. Celebrate each season and holiday with a splash of color. Spring into spring with an explosion of flowers and spring scenes. Sail into summer with photos of foreign lands and water sports. Slide into the winter season with snow scenes. An especially attractive bulletin board dressed up for the season attracts attention, livens up the atmosphere, and is very aesthetically pleasing.

87. Regional Releases

Feature a section of a bulletin board or a special corner with news articles of special interest to the community. These may be taken from the newspaper. Display notices of special regional celebrations and anniversaries. For example, January 6th is the "blessing of the sponge divers at Tarpon Springs, Florida." June 11th is Kamehameha Day in Hawaii. June 20th is West Virginia Day.

88. Word-Wise

Feature a word a day on the bulletin board. Use stick-on letters, which may be purchased at any school or office supplies store. Write the meaning of the word on an index card, and place it underneath the word.

Part IV
Fun with Book Lists

89. Boy Crazy

Find as many fiction titles in the library as you can with a boy's name.

1. *Abel's Island* (Steig.)
2. *Arabel and Mortimer* (Aiken.)
3. *Conrad's War* (Davies.)
4. *Java Jack* (Keele.)
5. *Jim and the Dolphin* (Butterworth.)
6. *Judge Benjamin: Superdog* (McInerney.)
7. *Old Jake and the Pirate's Treasure* (Hager.)
8. *Robinson Crusoe* (DeFoe.)
9. *Travels of Jamie* (McPheeters.)
10. *Gentle Ben* (Morey.)
11. *Max the Great* (Heath.)
12. *Michael Grows a Wish* (Lasell.)
13. *Wee Joseph* (MacKellar.)
14. *Adventures of Tom Sawyer* (Twain.)
15. *Billy Budd* (Melville.)
16. *David Copperfield* (Dickens.)
17. *Oliver Twist* (Dickens.)
18. *Uncle Tom's Cabin* (Stowe.)
19. *Adam Bede* (Eliot.)

90. Girl Crazy

Same as Boy Crazy, with girls' names.

1. *Kim* (Kipling.)
2. *Maudie and Me and the Dirty Book* (Miles.)
3. *Who Stole Kathy Young?* (Clark.)
4. *Horse Called Bonnie* (Van Tuyl.)
5. *Megan's Mare* (Hall.)
6. *Morgan for Melinda* (Gates.)
7. *Nicki and Wynne* (Morgenroth.)
8. *Anna Karenina* (Tolstoy.)
9. *Anne Frank: The Diary of a Young Girl* (Frank.)
10. *Annie* (Fleischer.)
11. *Jane Eyre* (Bronte.)
12. *Mary Poppins* (Travers.)
13. *Rebecca* (Du Maurier.)
14. *Alice's Adventures in Wonderland* (Carroll.)
15. *Emma* (Austen.)
16. *Sara Crewe* (Burnett.)
17. *Sister Carrie* (Dreiser.)
18. *What Katy Did* (Coolidge.)
19. *Dear Lola* (Angell.)
20. *Ellen Grae and Lady Ellen Grae* (Cleaver.)
21. *Deenie* (Blume.)
22. *Kathleen, Please Come Home* (O'Dell.)
23. *Lottery Rose* (Hunt.)
24. *Naomi in the Middle* (Klein.)
25. *Sarah Bishop* (O'Dell.)

91. Arbor Day

Same as Boy Crazy, with names of trees (or words such as "tree" or "forest").

1. *The Jungle Book* (Kipling.)
2. *House Without a Christmas Tree* (Rock.)
3. *Santa's Christmas Tree* (Weiler.)
4. *Bend to the Willow* (Bradley.)

 5. *Secret Lover of Elmtree* (Roth.)
 6. *The Elephant Tree* (Luger.)
 7. *Blue Willow* (Gates.)
 8. *Crimson Oak* (Almedingen.)
 9. *The Lady of the Linden Tree* (Picard.)
10. *Quickenberry Tree* (Motley.)
11. *Trace Through the Forest* (Robinson.)
12. *Valley of the Broken Cherry Trees* (Namioka.)
13. *Weeping Ash* (Aiken.)
14. *Phantom of Dark Oaks* (Sheldon.)
15. *View from the Cherry Tree* (Roberts.)
16. *Willow Pattern* (Van Gulik.)
17. *Miss Hickory* (Bailey.)
18. *The Dragon Tree* (Tooze.)
19. *Justice at Peachtree* (Marger.)
20. *The Taste of Spruce Gum* (Jackson.)
21. *Integral Trees* (Niven.)
22. *Bones on Black Spruce Mountain* (Budbill.)
23. *Sycamore Year* (Lee.)
24. *The Mulberry Music* (Orgel.)
25. *The Mimosa Tree* (Cleaver.)

92. Precious Gems

Same as Boy Crazy, with names of gems, precious metals, or minerals (or words such as "rock" or "stone").

 1. *The Diamond Smugglers* (Butterworth.)
 2. *Diamonds in the Dirt* (Campbell.)
 3. *Mystery of Chimney Rock* (Packard.)
 4. *Over Sea, Under Stone* (Cooper.)
 5. *Perilous Gold* (Wibberley.)
 6. *Rogue Diamond* (Lynne.)
 7. *Single Pebble* (Hersey.)
 8. *Black Pearl* (O'Dell.)
 9. *The Diamond in the Window* (Langton.)
10. *Mont Cant Gold* (Fisher.)
11. *The Silver Curlew* (Farjeon.)
12. *Silver on the Tree* (Cooper.)
13. *Truth about Stone Hollow* (Snyder.)

14. *The Walking Stones* (Hunter.)
15. *White Gold Wielder* (Donaldson.)
16. *Crystal Cornerstone* (Beers.)
17. *Gold-lined Box* (Hall.)
18. *Rough Diamond* (Fish.)
19. *Streets of Gold* (Branson.)
20. *Emerald* (Whitney.)
21. *Mystery of the Black Diamonds* (Whitney.)
22. *Secret of the Stone Face* (Whitney.)
23. *House Upon a Rock* (Pedersen.)
24. *Ironhead* (Ellis.)

93. Holiday Cheer

Same as Boy Crazy, with names of holidays.

1. *Easter Egg Hunt* (Freeman.)
2. *Halloween Party* (Christie.)
3. *Twelve Deaths of Christmas* (Babson.)
4. *Halloween Tree* (Bradbury.)
5. *Roadside Valentine* (Adler.)
6. *A Christmas Carol* (Dickens.)
7. *Christmas Memory* (Capote.)
8. *House Without a Christmas Tree* (Rock.)
9. *Night Before Christmas* (Moore.)
10. *Santa's Christmas Tree* (Weiler.)
11. *This Way to Christmas* (Sawyer.)
12. *The Best Christmas Pageant Ever* (Robinson.)

94. Spring Bouquet

Same as Boy Crazy, with names of flowers and plants.

1. *Clover* (Coolidge.)
2. *Effect of Gamma Rays on Man-in-the-Moon Marigolds* (Zindel.)
3. *Lottery Rose* (Hunt.)
4. *Where the Lilies Bloom* (Cleaver.)
5. *The Liberation of Tansy Warner* (Tolan.)

6. *Lilac Night* (Hinkemeyer.)
7. *The Coriander* (Dillon.)
8. *Golden Daffodils* (Gould.)
9. *Under the Mistletoe* (Mathews.)
10. *Dandelion Wine* (Bradbury.)
11. *God Bless You, Mr. Rosewater* (Vonnegut.)
12. *Lotus Caves* (Christopher.)
13. *Crocuses Were Over, Hitler Was Dead* (Symon.)
14. *Blood Root Flower* (Callaway.)
15. *Wild Violets* (Green.)
16. *Sign of the Chrysanthemum* (Paterson.)
17. *Have You Seen Hyacinth Macaw* (Giff.)
18. *The Street of the Flower Boxes* (Mann.)
19. *Smile Like a Plastic Daisy* (Levitin.)
20. *Diving for Roses* (Windsor.)
21. *Amen, Moses Gardenia* (Ferris.)

95. Animal Farm

Same as Boy Crazy, with names of animals.

1. *Albatross* (Anthony.)
2. *Bearcat* (Johnson.)
3. *The Black Stallion* (Farley.)
4. *Calm Horse, Wild Night* (Cohen.)
5. *Curse of Camp Gray Owl* (Clyne.)
6. *Dear Rat* (Cunningham.)
7. *Dogwalker* (Burnham.)
8. *House at Gray Eagle* (MacDonald.)
9. *One Hundred and One Dalmatians* (Smith.)
10. *In the Shadow of the Bear* (St. George.)
11. *Jim and the Dolphin* (Butterworth.)
12. *Judge Benjamin: Superdog* (McInerney.)
13. *Just a Dog* (Griffiths.)
14. *The Leopard's Tooth* (Kotzwinkle.)
15. *Night of the Wolf* (Bryan.)
16. *Of Nightingales That Weep* (Paterson.)
17. *Operation Cobra* (Bodelson.)
18. *Rumble Fish* (Hinton.)
19. *Seventh Raven* (Dickinson.)

20. *Snowshoe Trek to Otter River* (Budbill.)
21. *Tarzan, King of the Apes* (Vinge.)
22. *Tiger Rose* (Eisenberg.)
23. *Touch Not the Cat* (Stewart.)
24. *Watchdogs of Abaddon* (Melchior.)
25. *Winter of the White Seal* (Herbert.)

96. Pigments and Tints

Same as Boy Crazy, with names of colors.

1. *The Black Stallion* (Farley.)
2. *Blackbeard's Ghost* (Stahl.)
3. *Black Symbol* (Johnson.)
4. *Black Tide* (Innes.)
5. *Curse of Camp Gray Owl* (Clyne.)
6. *House at Gray Eagle* (MacDonald.)
7. *Hunters of the Black Swamp* (Harnish-Feger.)
8. *Out of the Blue* (McManus.)
9. *Perilous Gold* (Wibberley.)
10. *Silhouette in Scarlet* (Peters.)
11. *Tiger Rose* (Eisenberg.)
12. *Where the Red Fern Grows* (Rawls.)
13. *White Fang* (London.)
14. *Winter of the White Seal* (Herbert.)
15. *Big Red* (Kjelgaard.)
16. *Black Beauty* (Sewell.)
17. *Blue Canyon Horse* (Clark.)
18. *Black Lobo* (Warren.)
19. *Irish Red* (Kjelgaard.)
20. *The Orange Scarf* (Geisert.)
21. *Outlaw Red: Son of Big Red* (Kjelgaard.)
22. *Green Mansions* (Hudson.)
23. *Scarlet Letter* (Hawthorne.)
24. *Tistou of the Green Thumb* (Dryon.)

97. Fast Food Freak

Same as Boy Crazy, with names of foods.

1. *Easter Egg Hunt* (Freeman.)
2. *Fast-Food King* (Eisenberg.)
3. *I Am the Cheese* (Cormier.)
4. *I Would Rather Be a Turnip* (Cleaver.)
5. *The Pistachio Prescription* (Danziger.)
6. *Raspberry One* (Terry.)
7. *The Animal, the Vegetable, and John D. Jones* (Byars.)
8. *Pumpkin Shell* (Forman.)
9. *Superfudge* (Blume.)
10. *The Enormous Egg* (Butterworth.)
11. *The Sea Egg* (Boston.)
12. *The Peppermint Pig* (Bawden.)
13. *Soup* (Peck.)
14. *Bread and Butter Journey* (Colver.)
15. *Kate Crackernuts* (Briggs.)
16. *Welcome Home, Jellybean* (Shyer.)
17. *Ginger Pye* (Estes.)
18. *Onion John* (Krumgold.)
19. *On the Banks of Plum Creek* (Wilder.)
20. *A Poppy in the Corn* (Weaver.)
21. *Justice at Peachtree* (Marger.)
22. *The Gumdrop Necklace* (LaFarge.)
23. *The Peppersalt Land* (Harris.)
24. *Striped Ice Cream* (Lexau.)
25. *The Taste of Spruce Gum* (Jackson.)

98. Winter Wonderland

Same as Boy Crazy, with words about winter.

1. *Winter of the White Seal* (Herbert.)
2. *Tough Winter* (Lawson.)
3. *Winter of the Owl* (Hanson.)
4. *London Snow: A Christmas Story* (Theroux.)
5. *Snowbound* (Mazer.)
6. *Birds of Winter* (Vrettos.)
7. *Kim's Winter* (Wyatt.)
8. *Absolute Zero* (Cresswell.)
9. *Cold Feet* (Leroy.)

10. *The Iceberg and Its Shadow* (Greenberg.)
11. *The Cricket Winter* (Holman.)
12. *Giant Cold* (Dickinson.)
13. *The Snowbird* (Calvert.)
14. *Wilderness Winter* (Thompson.)
15. *Avalanche* (Van Der Loeff.)
16. *Snowbound* (Aurembou.)
17. *The Tacky Little Icicle Shack* (Koob.)
18. *Winter Cottage* (Brink.)
19. *Winter of the Whale* (Carse.)
20. *Iceberg Hermit* (Roth.)
21. *Winter Thunder* (Sandoz.)
22. *Blind in the Snow* (Shyer.)
23. *Winter Grass* (Wheeler.)

99. Salute to Summer

Same as Boy Crazy, with words about summer.

1. *Beachcombers* (Cresswell.)
2. *Black Tide* (Innes.)
3. *Bugs* (Roszak.)
4. *Dive for the Sun* (Love.)
5. *Maybe Next Summer* (Schellie.)
6. *Summer in the South* (Marshall.)
7. *Summer of the Stallion* (Hanson.)
8. *Summer Secrets* (Glaser.)
9. *Summer Girls, Love Boys* (Mazer.)
10. *Summer of Fear* (Duncan.)
11. *Sunshine* (Kerr.)
12. *Birds of Summer* (Snyder.)
13. *Footlight Summer* (Chambers.)
14. *The Night Swimmers* (Byers.)
15. *It's Summertime, It's Tuffy* (Angell.)
16. *A Summer's Lease* (Sachs.)
17. *Indian Summer* (Monjo.)
18. *Refugee Summer* (Fenton.)
19. *Summer of My German Soldier* (Greene.)
20. *One Special Summer* (Clayton.)
21. *A Summer Adventure* (Lewis.)

22. *Lost Summer* (Oppenheimer.)
23. *Seventeenth Summer* (Daly.)
24. *Summer Breezes* (Blake.)

100. Autumn Ambiance

Same as Boy Crazy, with words about autumn.

1. *Pumpkin Shell* (Forman.)
2. *Bad Fall* (Crawford.)
3. *Seedtime and Harvest* (Pearce.)
4. *Halloween Party* (Christie.)
5. *When the Leaves Begin to Fall* (Malmgren.)
6. *If the Earth Falls In* (Clark.)
7. *Autumn Street* (Lowry.)
8. *Early Autumn: A Spenser Novel* (Parker.)
9. *Free Fall in Crimson* (MacDonald.)

101. Spring Fever

Same as Boy Crazy, with words about spring.

1. *Believe In Spring* (Conrad.)
2. *Spring Begins in March* (Little.)
3. *Spring Love* (Sarasin.)
4. *The Spring of the Tiger* (Holt.)
5. *Come Spring* (Lewitt.)
6. *Wellspring* (Hawkins.)

102. Star Gazing

Same as Boy Crazy, with words pertaining to astronomy ("star, "planet," etc.).

1. *Delta Star* (Wambaugh.)
2. *Falling Star* (Eisenberg.)
3. *Neptune Rising* (Yolen.)
4. *In the Days of the Comet* (Wells.)

5. *Is There Life on a Plastic Planet* (Ames.)
6. *Night Without the Stars* (Howe.)
7. *Citizen of the Galaxy* (Heinlein.)
8. *Day of the Starwind* (Hill.)
9. *Dinosaur Planet* (McCaffrey.)
10. *Hitchhiker's Guide to the Galaxy* (Adams.)
11. *Lost Star* (Hoover.)
12. *Making the Representative for Planet 8* (Lessing.)
13. *Mysterious Planet* (Del Rey.)
14. *Orphan Star* (Foster.)
15. *Outpost Jupiter* (Del Rey.)
16. *Planet of Exile* (LeGuin.)
17. *Planet of the Apes* (Boulle.)
18. *Planet of the Warlord* (Hill.)
19. *Planet Out of the Past* (Collier.)
20. *Red Planet* (Heinlein.)
21. *Sands of Mars* (Clarke.)
22. *Starburst* (Pohl.)
23. *Star Chase* (Royal.)
24. *Star Ka'at* (Norton.)
25. *Aurora* (Smith.)

103. Sunny Days

Same as Boy Crazy, with the word "sun."

1. *Dive for the Sun* (Love.)
2. *Flag for Sunrise* (Stone.)
3. *Jim and the Sun Goddess* (Butterworth.)
4. *Evil Under the Sun* (Christie.)
5. *Sunshine* (Kerr.)
6. *The Shadow on the Sun* (Harris.)
7. *Dark Is the Sun* (Farmer.)
8. *Naked Sun* (Asimov.)
9. *Shadow on the Sun* (Paige.)

104. Moonglow

Same as Boy Crazy, with the word "moon."

1. *Effect of Gamma Rays on Man-in-the-Moon Marigolds* (Zindel.)
2. *Moon's on Fire* (Donaldson.)
3. *Moon on a String* (Springstubb.)
4. *Promise of Moonstone* (Engebrecht.)
5. *Moon and Me* (Irwin.)
6. *Lords of the Triple Moons* (Mayhar.)
7. *Many Moons* (Thurber.)
8. *Moonclock* (Von Cannon.)
9. *Sing Down the Moon* (O'Dell.)
10. *Time of the Hunter's Moon* (Holt.)
11. *Bad Moon* (Bromley.)
12. *Glimpses of the Moon* (Crispin.)
13. *Moon Eyes* (Poole.)
14. *The Moonstone* (Collins.)
15. *Panther's Moon* (Bond.)
16. *Half-a-Moon Inn* (Fleischman.)
17. *Alabama Moon* (Cole.)
18. *Moon Is Harsh Mistress* (Heinlein.)
19. *Moon of Mutiny* (Del Rey.)
20. *Sleepwalker's Moon* (Ellis.)
21. *Moonlight Bride* (Emecheta.)
22. *Search for the Crescent Moon* (Clifford.)
23. *Daughter of the Moon* (Maguire.)

105. Wanderlust

Same as Boy Crazy, but with names of places.

1. *Boys from Brazil* (Levin.)
2. *Bourne Identity* (Ludlum.)
3. *Hoard of the Himalayas* (Healey.)
4. *Honey of the Nile* (Berny.)
5. *Lost in the Shenandoahs* (Wilson.)
6. *The Temple of Mantos* (Butterworth.)
7. *Bridge Over the River Kwai* (Boulle.)
8. *Death on the Nile* (Christie.)
9. *Last Catholic in America* (Powers.)
10. *Escape from Paris* (Hart.)
11. *Green Hills of Africa* (Hemingway.)

12. *Horn of Africa* (Caputo.)
13. *Pacific Interlude* (Wilson.)
14. *Nobody Knows Me in Miami* (Klass.)
15. *Egypt Game* (Snyder.)
16. *Sabres of France* (Finn.)
17. *The Bombay Boomerang* (Dixon.)
18. *Mystery at the Moscow Fair* (Peters.)
19. *Mystery in Mexico* (Sheldon.)
20. *Mystery in Newfoundland* (Wees.)
21. *Red Sails to Capri* (Weil.)
22. *Strange Summer in Stratford* (Perez.)
23. *Trumpeter of Krakow* (Kelly.)
24. *Tombs of Atuan* (Le Guin.)
25. *Great Day in Holland* (Van Der Loeff.)

106. Island Escape

Same as Boy Crazy, but with the word "island."

1. *Abel's Island* (Steig.)
2. *Island* (Benchley.)
3. *The Island of Helos* (Butterworth.)
4. *Island of Dr. Moreau* (Wells.)
5. *Islands in the Stream* (Hemingway.)
6. *Island Keeper* (Mazer.)
7. *Island of the Blue Dolphins* (O'Dell.)
8. *Secret Island* (Moore.)
9. *Cutlass Island* (Corbett.)
10. *Golden Island* (Allfrey.)
11. *Big Blue Island* (Gage.)
12. *Halcyon Island* (Knowles.)
13. *Island* (Holland.)

107. Bird's-Eye View

Same as Boy Crazy, with names of birds.

1. *Albatross* (Anthony.)
2. *Of Nightingales That Weep* (Paterson.)

3. *Seventh Raven* (Dickinson.)
4. *Kilroy and the Gull* (Benchley.)
5. *Willie Was Different: The Tale of an Ugly Thrushing* (Rockwell.)
6. *Winter of the Owl* (Hanson.)
7. *Seabird* (Holling.)
8. *Sign of the Owl* (Chester.)
9. *The Snowbird* (Calbert.)
10. *The Clue of the Screeching Owl* (Dixon.)
11. *Raven's Cry* (Harris.)
12. *Goodbye, Dove Square* (McNeill.)
13. *No-Good Bird* (Burchardt.)
14. *Shadow of a Crow* (Pitcher.)
15. *The White Bird* (Bulla.)
16. *The White Lark* (Turnbull.)
17. *Red Bird of Ireland* (Langford.)
18. *White Sparrow* (Brown.)
19. *Before the Lark* (Brown.)
20. *The Sea Gull Woke Me* (Stolz.)
21. *Maltese Falcon* (Hammett.)
22. *One Flew Over the Cuckoo's Nest* (Kesey.)
23. *Birds of Winter* (Vrettos.)
24. *Once More the Hawks* (Hennessy.)
25. *I Heard the Owl Call My Name* (Craven.)

108. Network of Names

Same as Boy Crazy, but with last names.

1. *The Swiss Family Robinson* (Wyss.)
2. *Taking Care of Carruthers* (Marshall.)
3. *Travels of Jamie McPheeters* (Taylor.)
4. *Who Stole Kathy Young?* (Clark.)
5. *Dog Called Houdini* (Palmer.)
6. *Adventures of Huckleberry Finn* (Twain.)
7. *Adventures of Sherlock Holmes* (Doyle.)
8. *Anna Karenina* (Tolstoy.)
9. *Brothers Karamazov* (Dostoyevsky.)
10. *Billy Budd* (Melville.)
11. *Ben Hur* (Wallace.)

12. *David Copperfield* (Dickens.)
13. *Doctor Jekyll and Mr. Hyde* (Stevenson.)
14. *Doctor Zhivago* (Pasternak.)
15. *Don Quixote* (Cervantes.)
16. *Frankenstein* (Shelley.)
17. *Jane Eyre* (Bronte.)
18. *Little Lord Fauntleroy* (Burnett.)
19. *Mary Poppins* (Travers.)
20. *Oliver Twist* (Dickens.)
21. *Robinson Crusoe* (Defoe.)
22. *Adventures of Tom Sawyer* (Twain.)
23. *Alistair Maclean* (Maclean.)
24. *Allan Quatermain* (Haggard.)
25. *Elmer Gantry* (Lewis.)

109. Body Basics

Same as Boy Crazy, with parts of the body.

1. *Barefoot a Thousand Miles* (Gray.)
2. *Gay Neck* (Mukerji.)
3. *White Fang* (London.)
4. *Thunderhead* (O'Hara.)
5. *Eye of the Needle* (Follett.)
6. *Farewell to Arms* (Hemingway.)
7. *In Cold Blood* (Capote.)
8. *Hunchback of Notre Dame* (Hugo.)
9. *Pardon Me, You're Stepping on My Eyeball* (Zindel.)
10. *Stranger With My Face* (Duncan.)
11. *Barefoot Brigade* (Jones.)
12. *Razor Eyes* (Hough.)
13. *Tiger Eyes* (Blume.)
14. *Bloodroot Flower* (Callaway.)
15. *Dragon's Blood* (Yolen.)
16. *Heart's Blood* (Yolen.)
17. *Tistou of the Green Thumb* (Druon.)
18. *Wind Eye* (Westall.)
19. *A Five-Color Buick and a Blue-Eyed Cat* (Wood.)
20. *Bloody Country* (Collier.)

21. *Brother Dusty Feet* (Sutcliff.)
22. *Alice With the Golden Hair* (Hull.)
23. *Secret of the Stone Face* (Whitney.)

110. Wistful Winds

Same as Boy Crazy, with the word "wind."

1. *Gone With the Wind* (Mitchell.)
2. *No Promises in the Wind* (Hunt.)
3. *The Wind in the Willows* (Grahame.)
4. *Wind Eye* (Westall.)
5. *Bridle the Wind* (Aiken.)
6. *Orphans of the Wind* (Haugaard.)
7. *King of the Wind* (Henry.)
8. *Night Wind* (Allan.)
9. *Dawn Wind* (Sutcliff.)
10. *A Wind of Change* (Barnes.)

111. Winsome Witches

Same as Boy Crazy, with the word "witch."

1. *Witch Week* (Jones.)
2. *Witchwood* (Lukeman.)
3. *The Girl in the Witch House* (Halberg.)
4. *Witches' Bridge* (Carleton.)
5. *Witches' Children* (Clapp.)
6. *Witch of Blackbird Pond* (Speare.)
7. *The Witch's Daughter* (Bawden.)
8. *Witches of Worm* (Snyder.)
9. *Witch's Sister* (Naylor.)

112. Captivating Caverns

Same as Boy Crazy, with the word "caves."

1. *Clan of the Cave Bear* (Auel.)

2. *The Cave Above Delphi* (Corbett.)
3. *Cave-In* (Dixon.)
4. *Cave of Danger* (Walton.)
5. *Caves of Fire and Ice* (Murphy.)
6. *Caves of Steel* (Asimov.)
7. *Lotus Caves* (Christopher.)

113. Array of Abbreviations

Same as Boy Crazy, with abbreviations.

1. *Dr. Jekyll and Mr. Hyde* (Stevenson.)
2. *E.T., the Extra-Terrestrial* (Kotzwinkle.)
3. *H.E.L.P.* (Bonham.)
4. *It's O.K. If You Don't Love Me* (Klein.)
5. *SS-GB* (Deighton.)
6. *XPD* (Deighton.)
7. *Island of Dr. Moreau* (Wells.)
8. *Mrs. Frisby and the Rats of NIMH* (O'Brien.)
9. *Philip Birdsong's ESP* (Lawrence.)
10. *Voyage of QV66* (Lively.)
11. *The Turtle Street Trading Co.* (Klevin.)
12. *Men from P.I.G. and R.O.B.O.T.* (Harrison.)
13. *Miss P. and Me* (McNeil.)
14. *CF in His Corner* (Radley.)
15. *IOU's* (Sebestyen.)
16. *Annabelle Starr, E.S.P.* (Perl.)
17. *M.V. Sexton Speaking* (Newton.)

114. Stormy Weather

Same as Boy Crazy, with words about storms and bad weather.

1. *Typhoon* (Conrad.)
2. *You Are the Rain* (Knudson.)
3. *Rain Boat* (Kendall.)
4. *Thunder on the Tennessee* (Wisler.)
5. *Storm Without Rain* (Adkins.)

6. *Fog* (Lee.)
7. *Rainsong* (Whitney.)
8. *Roll of Thunder, Hear My Cry* (Taylor.)
9. *Acid Rain* (Boyle.)
10. *Storm from the West* (Willard.)
11. *Winter Thunder* (Sandoz.)
12. *Iceberg Hermit* (Roth.)
13. *Earthquake 2099* (Sullivan.)
14. *Blood in the Snow* (Shyer.)
15. *Unicorns in the Rain* (Cohen.)

115. Shortcuts

Same as Boy Crazy, with contractions.

1. *It's Not the End of the World* (Blume.)
2. *It's O.K. If You Don't Love Me* (Klein.)
3. *It's Not What You Expect* (Klein.)
4. *Then Again, Maybe I Won't* (Blume.)
5. *What It's All About* (Klein.)
6. *In Real Life I'm Just Kate* (Morgenroth.)
7. *And Then There'll Be Fireworks* (Elgin.)
8. *Time's Up* (Heide.)

116. Cat's-Eye

Same as Boy Crazy, with cats (including lions, tigers, etc.).

1. *The Leopard's Tooth* (Kotzwinkle.)
2. *Tiger Rose* (Eisenberg.)
3. *Cat Who Went to Heaven* (Coatsworth.)
4. *Tiger Eyes* (Blume.)
5. *Mystery of the Fat Cat* (Bonham.)
6. *Sea Leopard* (Thomas.)
7. *Tiger, the Lurp Dog* (Miller.)
8. *Time Cat* (Alexander.)
9. *Town Cats and Other Tales* (Alexander.)
10. *Shadow Like a Leopard* (Levoy.)
11. *Leopard* (Lampedusa.)

12. *Shield of the Three Lions* (Kaufman.)
13. *Spring of the Tiger* (Holt.)
14. *Village of the Vampire Cat* (Namioka.)
15. *The Clue of the Black Cat* (Berna.)
16. *Mystery at Lion's Gate* (Hall.)
17. *It's Like This Cat* (Neville.)
18. *The Boy Who Played Tiger* (Garlan.)
19. *Space Cats* (Kroll.)
20. *Cat That Was Left Behind* (Adler.)
21. *Cat Ate My Gymsuit* (Danziger.)
22. *Tiger in the Lake* (Kurkul.)

117. Saga of the Sea

Same as Boy Crazy, with words about the sea.

1. *Black Tide* (Innes.)
2. *Beast on the Brink* (Levin.)
3. *Beachcombers* (Cresswell.)
4. *From Thunder Bay* (Maling.)
5. *Gulf Stream North* (Conrad.)
6. *Over Sea, Under Stone* (Cooper.)
7. *Sea Story* (Johnston.)
8. *20,000 Leagues Under the Sea* (Verne.)
9. *Watership Down* (Adams.)
10. *The Deep* (Benchley.)
11. *Sea Wolf* (London.)
12. *Sea Leopard* (Thomas.)
13. *Heir of Sea and Fire* (McKillip.)
14. *Seaward* (Cooper.)
15. *The Sea Egg* (Boston.)
16. *Seabird* (Holling.)
17. *Sea Captain from Salem* (Wibberly.)
18. *Death Beside the Sea* (Babson.)
19. *Shen of the Sea* (Chrisman.)
20. *The Tide in the Attic* (Van Rhijin.)
21. *Across the Sea of Suns* (Benford.)
22. *Sea Change* (Burchard.)
23. *The Sea Gull Woke Me* (Stolz.)
24. *Taro and the Sea Turtles* (Dobrin.)

118. Nightly Narratives

Same as Boy Crazy, with the word "night."

1. *Calm Horse, Wild Night* (Cohen.)
2. *Night of the Running Man* (Wells.)
3. *Night of the Wolf* (Bryan.)
4. *Fly-By-Night* (Peyton.)
5. *Night Before Christmas* (Moore.)
6. *Night in Distant Motion* (Korschunow.)
7. *Night Sky* (Francis.)
8. *Crystal Nights* (Murray.)
9. *Good Night, Mr. Tom* (Magorian.)
10. *The Night Gift* (McKillip.)
11. *Night Journeys* (Avi.)
12. *Night Shift* (King.)
13. *Nightmare Ship* (Richardson.)
14. *Nightscape* (Chastain.)
15. *Night Landings* (Prince.)
16. *Nightmare Store* (Milton.)
17. *Night of Fire and Blood* (Kelley.)
18. *Night of the Werewolf* (Dixon.)
19. *Night She Died* (Simpson.)
20. *Night Spider Case* (Baker.)
21. *Night Wind* (Allan.)
22. *Night Without Stars* (Howe.)
23. *Campfire Nights* (Cowan.)
24. *Night of the Prom* (Spector.)

119. Horror Show

Same as Boy Crazy, but with horror words ("death," "terror," etc.).

1. *Border Kidnap* (Marks.)
2. *Death Tour* (Michael.)
3. *River of Death* (Maclean.)
4. *Savage Journey* (Eckert.)
5. *Prelude to Terror* (MacInnes.)

6. *Executioner's Song* (Mailer.)
7. *Hell's Kitchen* (Appel.)
8. *Killing Mr. Griffin* (Duncan.)
9. *Nightmare Ship* (Richardson.)
10. *Suicide Course* (Brown.)
11. *Kidnapping of Christina Lattimore* (Nixon.)
12. *Doomsday Gang* (Platt.)

120. Malaise

Same as Boy Crazy, with words about illness or injury.

1. *Altered States* (Chayefsky.)
2. *Fever* (Cook.)
3. *Finding Fever* (Baird.)
4. *Coma* (Cook.)
5. *Terminal Man* (Crichton.)
6. *Phaedra Complex* (Eyerly.)
7. *Cold Feet* (Leroy.)
8. *In Cold Blood* (Capote.)
9. *Giant Cold* (Dickinson.)
10. *Bad Fall* (Crawford.)
11. *Save the Loonies* (Milton.)
12. *Silent Voice* (Cunningham.)
13. *Fevre Dream* (Martin.)
14. *Twice Burned* (Gettel.)
15. *Lunatic Fringe* (DeAndrea.)
16. *Love Lies Bleeding* (Crispin.)
17. *Kneeknock Rise* (Babbitt.)
18. *The Paleface Redskins* (Jackson.)
19. *Year of Sweet Senior Insanity* (Levitin.)

121. Shades of Green

Same as Boy Crazy, with shades of green.

1. *A Stranger at Green Knowe* (Boston.)
2. *Green Hills of Africa* (Hemingway.)
3. *Mrs. Fish, Ape, and Me, the Dump Green* (Mazer.)

4. *The Pistachio Prescription* (Danziger.)
5. *Dark Green Tunnel* (Eckert.)
6. *The River at Green Knowe* (Boston.)
7. *Tistou of the Green Thumb* (Druon.)
8. *Treasure of Green Knowe* (Boston.)
9. *How Green Was My Valley* (Llewellyn.)
10. *Jade Amulet* (Linton.)
11. *Jade* (Watson.)
12. *Lady Jade* (O'Grady.)
13. *Death in the Greenhouse* (Anderson.)
14. *An Enemy at Green Knowe* (Boston.)
15. *Susannah and the Poison Green Halloween* (Elmore.)
16. *Anne of Green Gables* (Montgomery.)
17. *Green Grow the Rushes* (Lyon.)
18. *A Pistol in Greenyards* (Hunter.)
19. *Lavender-Green Magic* (Norton.)

122. Silver Streak

Same as Boy Crazy, with the word "silver."

1. *Silver Chief: Dog of the North* (O'Brien.)
2. *Silver Chair* (Lewis.)
3. *The Silver Curlew* (Farjeon.)
4. *Silver on the Tree* (Cooper.)
5. *Quicksilver Lady* (Whitehead.)
6. *By the Shores of Silver Lake* (Wilder.)
7. *The Silver Branch* (Sutcliff.)
8. *Silvery Past* (Ranson.)
9. *Robert Silverberg Omnibus* (Silverberg.)
10. *The Silver Crown* (O'Brien.)
11. *Girl with the Silver Eyes* (Roberts.)
12. *Silver Coach* (Adler.)

123. Sultry Story

Same as Boy Crazy, with words about fire and heat.

1. *Flameout* (Jackson.)
2. *Friend Fire and the Dark Wings* (Fyson.)
3. *Chariots of Fire* (Weatherby.)
4. *Inferno* (Dante.)
5. *Fireweed* (Walsh.)
6. *Moon's on Fire* (Donaldson.)
7. *And Then There'll Be Fireworks* (Elgin.)
8. *A Firefly Named Torchy* (Waber.)
9. *Firelings* (Kendall.)
10. *Heir of Sea and Fire* (McKillip.)
11. *Wing and the Flame* (Hanlon.)
12. *Hell's Kitchen* (Appel.)
13. *Fire from Heaven* (Renault.)
14. *Firestarter* (King.)
15. *Twice Burned* (Gettel.)
16. *Marked by Fire* (Thomas.)
17. *Glass Flame* (Whitney.)
18. *Night of Fire and Blood* (Kelley.)
19. *Rat on Fire* (Higgins.)
20. *Firedragon* (Benezra.)
21. *The Nearest Fire* (Wilder.)
22. *Pool of Fire* (Christopher.)
23. *Fireball* (Christopher.)
24. *Dance Around the Fire* (Cone.)
25. *Frozen Fire* (Houston.)
26. *Caves of Fire and Ice* (Murphy.)

124. Cast of Cinnabar

Same as Boy Crazy, with shades of red.

1. *Silhouette in Scarlet* (Peters.)
2. *Tiger Rose* (Eisenberg.)
3. *Where the Red Fern Grows* (Rawls.)
4. *Big Red* (Kjelgaard.)
5. *Irish Red* (Kjelgaard.)
6. *Outlaw Red: Son of Big Red* (Kjelgaard.)
7. *Red Badge of Courage* (Crane.)
8. *Redburn* (Melville.)
9. *The Red Pony* (Steinbeck.)

10. *The Scarlet Letter* (Hawthorne.)
11. *Lottery Rose* (Hunt.)
12. *Air Glow Red* (Slater.)
13. *Raspberry One* (Ferry.)
14. *Red Flight Two* (Dank.)
15. *Mr. Death and the Redheaded Woman* (Eustis.)
16. *Cinnamon Cane* (Pollowitz.)
17. *No Scarlet Ribbons* (Terris.)
18. *The Red Balloon* (Lamorisse.)
19. *Tarantula and the Red Chigger* (Robertson.)
20. *Crimson Oak* (Almedingen.)
21. *Strawberry Girl* (Lenski.)
22. *Red Pawns* (Wibberly.)
23. *When Hitler Stole Pink Rabbit* (Kerr.)
24. *Scarlet Pimpernel* (Orczy.)
25. *Scarlet Streamers* (Whitehouse.)
26. *Two Worlds of Coral Harpen* (Tarlton.)
27. *Vermillion* (Whitney.)
28. *Cinnamon Skin* (MacDonald.)
29. *Crimson Flame* (Dixon.)

125. Affairs of State

Same as Boy Crazy, with names of states.

1. *Green Grass of Wyoming* (O'Hara.)
2. *Mississippi Possum* (Miles.)
3. *Washington Square* (James.)
4. *Oregon at Last* (Vander Loeff.)
5. *Thunder on the Tennessee* (Wisler.)
6. *Alabama Moon* (Cole.)
7. *California Girl* (Quin-Harkin.)
8. *California* (Ross.)
9. *Californios* (L'Amour.)
10. *Colorado* (Ross.)
11. *Nebraska* (Ross.)
12. *Nevada* (Ross.)
13. *Oregon* (Ross.)
14. *Texas* (Ross.)
15. *Utah* (Ross.)

16. *Washington* (Ross.)
17. *Wyoming* (Ross.)
18. *A Connecticut Yankee in King Arthur's Court* (Twain.)
19. *Good Luck Arizona Man* (Benedict.)

126. Tincture of Blue

Same as Boy Crazy, with shades of blue.

1. *Out of the Blue* (McManus.)
2. *Blue Canyon Horse* (Clark.)
3. *Is That You Miss Blue?* (Kerr.)
4. *Island of the Blue Dolphins* (O'Dell.)
5. *Bright Blue Sky* (Hennessy.)
6. *Shelter on Blue Barns Road* (Adler.)
7. *Blue Adept* (Anthony.)
8. *Blue Sword* (McKinley.)
9. *Rhapsody in Blue of Mickey Kein* (Herman.)
10. *The Blue Hills* (Howe.)
11. *A Five-Color Buick and a Blue-Eyed Cat* (Wood.)
12. *The Blue and the Gray* (Leekley.)
13. *Blue Willow* (Gates.)
14. *Over the Blue Mountain* (Richter.)
15. *Prison Window, Jerusalem Blue* (Clements.)
16. *Zoar Blue* (Hickman.)
17. *Baby Blue Rip-Off* (Collins.)
18. *Solitary Blue* (Voigt.)
19. *Big Blue Island* (Gage.)
20. *Summer of the Sky-Blue Bikini* (Klevin.)
21. *Beyond the Blue Event Horizon* (Pohl.)
22. *Blue Denim Blues* (Smith.)
23. *Angel Dust Blues* (Strasser.)
24. *Blue Hills* (Howe.)
25. *Blues for Silk Garcia* (Tamar.)

127. Western Round-Up

Make a listing of as many western fiction titles as you can find in the library, or titles that have a western setting or flavor.

Have the students wear cowboy outfits and old western costumes.

1. *Allegiance* (Green.)
2. *Ambush* (Porter.)
3. *Bendigo Shafter* (L'Amour.)
4. *Buckskin Run* (L'Amour.)
5. *Defenders of Windhaven* (DeJourlet.)
6. *Fallon* (L'Amour.)
7. *Milo Talon* (L'Amour.)
8. *Lawless* (Jakes.)
9. *Kilrone* (L'Amour.)
10. *High Lonesome* (L'Amour.)
11. *Furies* (Jakes.)
12. *Man Called Noon* (L'Amour.)
13. *Massacre at Fall Creek* (West.)
14. *Law and Outlaw* (Vance.)
15. *I'll Tell You a Tale* (Dobie.)
16. *Renegade* (Porter.)
17. *Shane* (Schaefer.)
18. *Range Trouble* (Allen.)
19. *Mister, You Got Yourself a Horse* (Welsch.)
20. *Thirsty* (Dequasie.)
21. *Warlock* (Hall.)
22. *Winter Grass* (Wheeler.)
23. *Track of the Cat* (Clark.)
24. *Track of a Killer* (Overholser.)
25. *Western Hall of Fame* (Morrow.)

128. Contemporary Countdown

List as many fiction titles as you can find in the card catalog that have to do with figures.

1. *Eight Plus One* (Cormier.)
2. *Fifteen* (Cleary.)
3. *Crazy Eights* (Dana.)
4. *Double Wedding* (Du Jardin.)
5. *Five August Days* (Burton.)
6. *Half the Battle* (Hall.)

7. *I Was a 98-pound Duckling* (Van Leeuwen.)
8. *I've Missed a Sunset or Three* (Wood.)
9. *79 Squares* (Bosse.)
10. *You Can't Take Twenty Dogs on a Date* (Cavanna.)
11. *Cute Is a Four-Letter Word* (Pevsner.)
12. *First Affair* (Burchard.)
13. *Fourteen* (Sachs.)
14. *Five Summers* (Guernsey.)
15. *After the First Death* (Cormier.)

129. Questionable Tales

Find as many fiction titles as you can that are questions.

1. *Anybody Home?* (Fisher.)
2. *Is That You Miss Blue?* (Kerr.)
3. *How Far Is Berkeley?* (Chetin.)
4. *What's the Matter with the Dobsons?* (Colman.)
5. *Who's Hu?* (Namioka.)
6. *Is There a Life After Graduation, Henry Birnbaum?* (Balducci.)
7. *Do You See What I See?* (St. George.)
8. *Can I Get There by Candlelight?* (Doty.)
9. *Will the Real Renie Lake Please Stand Up?* (Morgenroth.)
10. *What Do You Do When Your Mouth Won't Open?* (Pfeffer.)
11. *Where Has Deedie Wooster Been All These Years?* (Jacobs.)
12. *Why Me? The Story of Jenny* (Dizenzo.)
13. *Are You There, God? It's Me, Margaret* (Blume.)
14. *How Can We Talk?* (Aydt.)
15. *Suzy Who?* (Madison.)

130. Fête of Book Lists

If your library has a microcomputer, you might be able to do this one very easily. If not, perhaps you have built up your repertoire of fiction and nonfiction book lists. Students may visit the library either with their class or individually. Book lists may be comprised of the library's holdings. Have various selections of fiction bibliographies in separate box compartments on the circulation counter or on tables. Student aides may assist students in locating lists and books.

131. Bibliography Session

Invite the school psychologist and the guidance counselors for a visit to the school library to discuss some problems teenagers must face. Prepare a list of fiction books that deal with such problems as well as a list of nonfiction books on death, family problems, unmarried mothers, runaway children, orphans, mental and emotional problems, physical handicaps, etc.

Part V
Reference Books

132. Where in the World?

Find out in what country each of the following is located (students may use *Webster's Geographical Dictionary*, G. & C. Merriam Co., 1967):

1. Busa. (Nigeria.)
2. Kansk. (Russia.)
3. Maltby. (England.)
4. Seabrook. (U.S. — New Hampshire.)
5. Tirol. (Austria.)
6. Leh. (India.)
7. Gravelines. (France.)
8. Gibraltar. (Spain.)
9. Bilecik. (Turkey.)
10. Luchow. (China.)
11. Suwo. (Japan.)
12. Young Island. (Antarctica.)
13. Les Saintes. (West Indies.)
14. Cegled. (Hungary.)
15. Cape Camaron. (Honduras.)
16. Martin Garcia. (Uruguay.)
17. Siljan. (Sweden.)
18. Mira. (Ecuador.)
19. Lakeland. (U.S. — Florida.)
20. Luembe. (Angola.)

133. Gifted Reference Sessions

The "gifted" students visit the library on numerous occasions. We hold a series of sessions beginning with the encyclopedia, the card catalog, and the *Reader's Guide to Periodical Literature*. For instance, we look at the *World Book*, *Britannica Junior*, and *Compton's* encyclopedias; how they are arranged; the index and cross references; key words; guide words and illustrations, charts; etc. With the card catalog, we examine the drawers; the *see* and *see also* references; the inside guides; the arrangement of cards in the catalog; the subject, title, and author cards, and analytic cards; and the Dewey Decimal System. We look at the *Reader's Guide*; its arrangement; the abbreviations and guide to periodical abbreviations; and a sample subject and author entry.

We look at primary, secondary, and tertiary knowledge; steps in the various reference process; and ways to zero in on what one is hunting for. We examine examples of reference sources such as bibliographies, indexes and abstracts, encyclopedias, subject encyclopedias, dictionaries, quotations, almanacs and special subject almanacs, yearbooks and annuals, directories, handbooks and manuals, biographical sources, geographical sources, statistical reference sources, and government documents. Students must complete a research project by using numerous types of reference tools.

134. Family Names

Find the meaning of the following family names using the *New Dictionary of American Family Names* (Elsdon C. Smith; Harper & Row, 1973).

1. Burns — (Eng.) dweller at a brook
2. Hwang — (Kor., Chin.) yellow
3. Reinhardt — (Ger.) descendant of Rinhardt, meaning counsel, hard
4. Gruodis — (Lith.) the roundish, ball-like man
5. Ansley — (Eng.) one who came from Ansley, a wood with a hermitage
6. Wenzel — (Ger.) descendant of Wenzel, a pet form of Wenzeslaus, meaning glory

7. Luby — (Pol., Rus., Ukr.) the dear beloved man
8. Gassin — (Fr.) dweller among oak trees
9. Tomasevich — (Rus.) the son of Tomas, Russian form of Thomas, meaning a twin
10. Kjoss — (Nor.) dweller in a narrow valley or at a narrow creek
11. Mort — (Fr., Eng.) one with a brown skin or dark complexion; a Moor
12. Huxley — (Eng.) one who came from Huxley, Hucci's grove in Cheshire
13. Deer — (Scot.) one who came from Deer (forest) in Aberdeershire
14. Naik — (Hindu) a leader
15. Kusaki — (Jap.) grass, tree
16. Marino — (It.) descendant of Marinor, meaning of the sea
17. Keats — (Eng.) descendant of Keat, meaning lively
18. Seth — (Heb.) descendant of Seth, meaning the appointed substitute
19. Hietala — (Finn.) dweller in a sandy place
20. Melas — (Gr.) the swarthy man, black
21. Ressler — (Ger.) one who raised and sold flowers
22. Hillstrom — (Swed.) boulder stream
23. Djuric — (Sl.) descendant of Djurik, a slovakian form of George, meaning farmer
24. Miles — (Wel.) descendant of Miles, meaning soldier
25. Kutt — (Estonian) one who hunted game

135. Doubleday Roget's Thesaurus

Using the *Doubleday Roget's Thesaurus in Dictionary Form* (Sidney Landau; Doubleday, 1977), find an antonym and a synonym for the following terms.

1. clever — S: adroit; A: clumsy.
2. besides — S: as well as; A: not including.
3. fragmentary — S: disconnected; A: unified.
4. portable — S: transportable; A: stationary.
5. iniquity — S: sinfulness; A: virtue.
6. proficient — S: capable; A: bungling.

7. vacuous — S: imbecilic; A: alert.
8. infringe — S: violate; A: obey.
9. dolt — S: nitwit; A: intellectual.
10. celestial — S: ethereal; A: earthy.

136. Reader's Encyclopedia

Using *The Reader's Encyclopedia* (William Rose Benet; Crowell, 1965), what or who are the following:

1. Huckleberry Finn? (a novel by Mark Twain.)
2. Uncle Tom's Cabin? (a novel by Harriet Beecher Stowe: a book about an old Negro slave.)
3. The Old Man and the Sea? (a novelette by Ernest Hemingway about an old Cuban fisherman who has has been out to sea for 84 days without a catch.)
4. Pierre Corneille? (1606–1684: French dramatist.)
5. Cordelia? (in Shakespeare's *King Lear*, the youngest daughter of Lear.)
6. Merlin? (a magician in Arthurian legend.)
7. Merope? (one of the Pleiades.)
8. Flying Dutchman? (a legendary ghost ship.)
9. Helios? (the Greek sun god.)
10. John Knox? (1505–1572: Scottish reformer & founder of Presbyterianism.)
11. Pleiades? (the most prominent cluster of stars in the constellation Taurus.)
12. Sense and Sensibility? (a novel by Jane Austen.)
13. South Wind? (a novel by Norman Douglas.)
14. The 42nd Parallel? (a novel by John Dos Passos.)
15. Neptune? (the Roman god of the sea.)

137. Believe It or Not

Decide whether the following is true or false by using the *Guinness Book of World Records* (Norris McWhirter; Sterling, 198—).

1. The hottest flame that can be produced is from car-

bon subnitride which at one atmosphere pressure is calculated to reach 5,261 K. (True.)

2. The greatest reliable age recorded for a dog is 29 years 5 months for a Queensland "heeler" named "Bluey" in Australia. (True.)

3. The highest speed reached in a nonmechanical sport is in skydiving, in which a speed of 200 mph is attained in a head-down free-falling position. (False.)

4. Most successful criminal lawyer: Sir Lionel Luckhoo of Guyana has 236 acquittals vs. 0 convictions in his career so far. (True.)

5. Fastest road motorcycle: the highest speed returned in an independent road test for a catalogued road machine is 190 mph for a Dunstall Suzuki GS 1000. (False.)

6. The largest recorded crystal of gem quality was a 520,000 carat (229 lb.) aquamarine found near Marambaia, Brazil in 1920. It yielded over 200,000 carats of gem-quality cut stones. (False.)

7. The largest camera ever built is the 30¼-ton Rolls-Royce camera built for Product Support (Graphics) Ltd. of Derby, England, completed in 1959. It measures 8 ft. 10 in. high, 8 ft. 3 in. wide, and 35 ft. long. (True.)

8. The tallest iceberg sighted off Greenland was 770 ft. high. (False.)

9. The tree most distant from any other tree is believed to be one at an oasis in the Ténéré Desert, Niger Republic. No other trees are within 31 miles. (True.)

10. The most expensive hotel accommodations are in the Celestial Suite on the ninth floor of the Astro Village Hotel, Houston, Texas, which is rented for $3,000 a day. This compares with the official New York City Presidential Suite in the Waldorf-Astoria at $1,900 a day. (True.)

11. The longest-lasting rainbow was for over 4 hours, and was reported from North Wales on August 14, 1979. (False.)

12. The largest mirage on record was that sighted in the Arctic at 83 N° 103 W° in 1913. (True.)

13. A candle 80 ft. high and 8½ ft. in diameter was

exhibited at the 1897 Stockholm Exhibition. (True.)
14. The largest restaurant chain is McDonald's Corp. in Oakbrook, Ill., founded April 16, 1955. (False.)
15. In March 1980, a divorce was reported in the Los Los Angeles Superior Court of California between Bernardine & Leopold Delper; both parties were 88 years old. (True.)

138. Science Search

Answer the following using the reference section of the library.

1. What is meant by "biotic factor"? (Plants are profoundly affected by various environmental factors, other plants and various animals, bacteria-weeds-fungus.) *Van Nostrand's Scientific Encyclopedia*, p. 193 (Van Nostrand, 1958). *Dictionary of Ecology*, p. 54 (Philosophical Library, 1962).

2. What is ecology? (The study of plants and animals in relation to their natural environment, including both physical features and living things. Ecology is a summing up, an attempt to fit each living thing into its place in the world — as an individual, as a member of a constantly changing community, and as a possible ancestor of new generations that will evolve by becoming adapted to their environmental conditions.) *Harper Encyclopedia of Science*, p. 351 (Harper & Row, 1967). *Dictionary of Ecology*, p. 121 (Philosophical Library, 1962).

3. What is meant by epithelium? (A sheet of cells that covers or lines organs, e.g. the skin and the lining of the gut.) *A Dictionary of Scientific Terms*, p. 25 (Ginn & Co., 1966).

4. Who first saw and described bacteria? (Anton Van Leeuwenhoek in the 17th century.) *Harper Encyclopedia of Science*, S.V. "bacteriology," p. 131 (Harper & Row, 1967).

5. What is a bacteriophage? What does it contain? (A virus that attacks bacterial cells, it contains DNA.) *The*

Harper Encyclopedia of Science. 1. 131 (Harper & Row, 1967).

6. What is the definition of nutrition? (The science of the chemicals living organisms need to take in to support their metabolism.) *New Encyclopedia of Science*, vol. 2, p. 249 (Raintree Pub., 1982).

7. If one bacterium were to divide every 20 minutes for 48 hours, how many descendants would there be? (Over 24 million million million million descendants.) *New Encyclopedia of Science*, vol. 2, S.V. "bacteria," p. 193 (Raintree Pub., 1982).

8. Who was the first to discover a simple form of learning in animals which he called "conditioning"? (Ivan Pavlov.) *New Encyclopedia of Science*, vol. 2, S.V. "learned behavior," p. 230 (Raintree Pub., 1982).

9. What is the form of learned behavior called imprinting? (The experience of an animal immediately after it is born influences the way it behaves.) *New Encyclopedia of Science*, vol. 2, S.V. "learned behavior or imprinting," p. 230 (Raintree Pub., 1982).

10. What treatment is used to kill cancer cells? (radiotherapy.) *New Encyclopedia of Science*, vol. 12, p. 1617 (Raintree, 1982).

11. The surface layer of the epidermis is made up of about how many layers of very flat cells, which are in fact dead? (20 layers.) *New Encyclopedia of Science*, vol. 13, p. 1803 (Raintree, 1982).

12. Why is not much known about the ecology of the desert? (Because the environment challenges the tolerance of human observers, and because funding organizations have been as unimpressed with this nonproductive land as the average citizen.) *Science: A New York Times Survey*, vol. 1, p. 246 (Arno Press, 1982).

13. What is a problem with some diseases today when antibiotics are given? (Resistance.) *Science: A New York Times Survey*, vol. 3, p. 183 (Arno Press, 1982).

14. What are the three different processes by which cellulosic manmade fibres are made? (The viscose process, the cuprammonium process, and the acetate process.) *The Way Things Work: An Illustrated Encyclopedia of*

Technology, p. 370 (Simon & Schuster, 1967).

15. What are the general symptoms of stomach cancer? (General symptoms: loss of weight, strength, or appetite, particularly for meat; fullness and gas after eating; discomfort over abdomen. In later stages when fully developed, cancer can be felt through abdominal walls.) *Fishbein's Illustrated Medical and Health Encyclopedia*, vol. 4, p. 1357 (H.S. Stuttman Co., Inc., 1977).

16. What is the origin of the chinese primrose? (Origin is obscure.) *The Pictorial Encyclopedia of Plants and Flowers*, p. 141 (Crown, 1966).

17. What is the hunter's moon? (The full moon following the harvest moon. Since harvest moon usually occurs in the last part of September in the northern hemisphere, hunter's moon is seen in October.) *The Amateur Astronomer's Glossary*, p. 58 (W.W. Norton & Co., 1967).

18. What is meant by "ley"? (An English term for land that is temporarily under grass, legumes, or mixtures of these.) *Dictionary of Ecology*, p. 204 (Philosophical Library, 1962).

19. What is the diameter of Uranus? (29,300 miles.) *Larousse Encyclopedia of Astronomy*, p. 224 (Paul Hamlyn, 1959).

20. What is a microorganism? (Any organism that is very small and must be viewed through a microscope, such as bacteria and some algae.) *Young People's Science Encyclopedia*, vol. 11, p. 1054 (Childrens Press, 1978).

21. What may a histamine sometimes be used for by physicians? (In testing stomach secretions.) *Compton's Illustrated Science Dictionary*, p. 281 (Encyclopaedia Britannica Educational Corporation, 1969).

22. What are the two distinct parts of the mature leaf? (The broadly expanded, thin green blade, and the petiole or stalk which supports it and connects it with the stem, a pair of outgrowths called stipules at base; blade-petiole-stipule.) *Van Nostrand's Scientific Encyclopedia*, p. 957 (Van Nostrand, 1958).

23. A pound of purified interferon was once estimated to be worth how much? ($20 billion.) *Science: A New*

York Times Survey, vol. 6, p. 130 (Arno Press, 1982).
24. What is gray water a sign of in aquariums? (Of over-feeding.) *Handbook of Tropical Aquarium Fishes*, p. 74 (T.F.H. Publications, 1971).
25. How long did it take for the volcano Vesuvius to bury Pompeii? (Thirty hours.) *Science: A New York Times Survey*, vol. 3, p. 59 (Arno Press, 1982).

139. Social Studies Search

Answer the following using the reference section of the library.

1. What is the earliest recorded eruption of Vesuvius, a volcano that destroyed Pompeii? (A.D. 79.) *1980 World Almanac*, p. 32 (Newspaper Enterprise Associated). *Lands and People*, vol. 4, p. 128 (Grolier, 1973). *National Geographic Index*, Nov. 1961, pp. 651–669 (National Geographic Society).
2. In the continent of Asia, the Dead Sea is how much below sea level? (about 1,300 ft. – 400m.) *Lands and People*, vol. 6, p. 364 (Grolier, 1973). *Webster's Geographical Dictionary*, p. 285 (G. & C. Merriam Co., 1967).
3. In Africa, what does the Suez Canal connect? (Red Sea with the Mediterranean.) *1980 World Almanac*, p. 533 (Newspaper Enterprise Associated). *Lands and People*, vol. 2, p. 57 (Grolier, 1967). *Webster's Geographical Dictionary*, p. 1090 (G. & C. Merriam Co., 1967).
4. When did Confucius live? (551 B.C.–479 B.C.) *Webster's Biographical Dictionary*, p. 539 (G. & C. Merriam Co., 1966). *The Encyclopedia of World History*, p. 45 (Houghton Mifflin, 1952). *1980 World Almanac*, p. 722 (Newspaper Enterprise Assoc.).
5. Who was Gandhi? (Hindu Nationalist leader, 1869–1948.) *Webster's Biographical Dictionary*, p. 574 (G. & C. Merriam Co., 1966). *Twentieth Century*, vol. 3, p. 281 (Purnell, 1979). *The Encyclopedia of World History*, p. 858 (Houghton Mifflin, 1952).

6. What actually is bamboo? (A grass.) *The Pictorial Encyclopedia of Plants and Flowers*, p. 558 (Crown, 1966). *Hammond's Nature Atlas of America*, p. 220 (Hammond, 1952).

7. Where can you find some information on pandas? *The Illustrated Encyclopedia of the Animal Kingdom*, vol. 1, p. 138 (Danbury Press, 1972). *The Illustrated Encyclopedia of the Animal Kingdom*, vol. 3, pp. 92–95 (Danbury Press, 1972). *The Living Earth*, p. 70 (Danbury Press, 1976).

8. How long ago was acupuncture known? (2800 B.C., in China.) *New Encyclopedia of Science*, p. 1390 (Raintree, 1982).

9. Where can one find information on Swahili? *(Lands and People*, vol. 1, pp. 14, 31, 312, 333, 335 [Grolier, 1973].)

10. Where can you find an article on diamonds? *(National Geographic Index*, Dec. 1950, pp. 779–80; Nov. 1952, pp. 695–712; April 1958, pp. 568–586; March 1952, pp. 321–362; March 1950, pp. 311–352.)

11. Where can you find information on silk? *(National Geographic Index*, June 1961, pp. 811–849.)

12. What is the name, date, and time of the first person to swim the English Channel? (Gertrude [Trudy] Ederle on Aug. 6, 1926. She swam from Gris-Nez, France, to Kingsdom [Dover], England, in 14 hours and 34 minutes.) *Famous First Facts*, p. 656 (H.W. Wilson Co., 1964).

13. What is the name and date of the first solo climb on Mt. Everest without oxygen? (May 29, 1953.) *Great Events of the 20th Century*, p. 419 (Reader's Digest Assoc., 1977). *Guinness Book of World Records*, p. 620 (Sterling).

14. What is the population of Kalamazoo, Mich.? (88,555 people in 1970.) *1980 World Almanac*, p. 215 (Newspaper Enterprise Assoc.).

15. What is the longitude and latitude of the North Magnetic Pole? (104 W 77 N.) *Compton's Illustrated Science Dictionary*, p. 395 (Encyclopaedia Britannica Educational Corp., 1969).

16. What is the date and location of the biggest recorded

tidal wave? (Aug. 1931, Huange He River, China.) *1980 World Almanac*, p. 749 (Newspaper Enterprise Assoc.).

17. What is the temperature, date, and location of the hottest temperature ever recorded? (136.4 F at Azizia, Libya, Africa, on Sept. 13, 1922.) *World Atlas, Rand McNally*, p. 197 (Rand McNally, 1968).

18. When and where did the ship *Titanic* sink? (British [White Star] liner hit iceberg on April 14–15, 1912, in the North Atlantic. 1,517 lives lost.) *1980 World Almanac*, p. 748 (Newspaper Enterprise Assoc.).

19. What are the names and date of the first men on the moon? (Neil Alden Armstrong and Buzz Aldrin.) *Footprints on the Moon*, p. 189.

20. What was the smallest boat to cross the Atlantic? (*Super Shrimp* — 18 ft., 4 in. Bermuda sloop. Aug. 1972–Aug. 1980.) *Guinness Book of World Records*, p. 326 (Sterling).

21. Who accomplished the first circumnavigation of the globe from the North Pole through the South Pole, and when? (The first flight was flown solo by Capt. Elgen M. Long, 44, in a piper Navajo, Nov. 5 to Dec. 3, 1971. He covered 38,896 miles in 215 flying hours. The cabin temperature sank to −40 F. over Antarctica.) *Guinness Book of World Records*, p. 326.

22. In the Lebanese Civil War, between whom is the basic conflict? (Syria and the Palestinians.) *The Great Contemporary Issues Series*, set I, vol. II, p. 428 (Arno Press, 1978).

23. When did knowledge of Africa open up? (Increased rapidly after the explorer Vasco da Gama opened a sea route to India in 1497.) *The McGraw-Hill Illustrated World History*, p. 219 (McGraw-Hill, 1964).

24. Find information on unemployment in China in modern times. (*The Great Contemporary Issues Series*, set I, vol. III, p. 537 [Arno Press, 1978].)

25. Find an article on yoga. ("Science Digest." 90:28-9. F 82. Hearst Corp.)

140. Webster's Geographical Dictionary

Find out what and where the following are, using the *Webster's Geographical Dictionary* (G. & C. Merriam Co., 1967).

1. Brandywine? (A creek in Pennsylvania and Delaware uniting with Christiana Creek at Wilmington, Delaware.)
2. Manchester Ship Canal? (A canal from Eastham, N.W. Cheshire, N.W. England, to Manchester.)
3. Tobago? (Island of the West Indies.)
4. Colima? (Volcano in Jalisco State, W. Central Mexico.)
5. Stonehenge? (An assemblage of upright stones on the Salisbury plain 7 miles north of Salisbury, England. Originally in 2 concentric circles enclosing 2 rows of smaller stones. Much uncertainty exists as to its origin and purpose.)
6. Lismore? (Island 9 miles long at entrance to Loch Linnhe, Argyll Co., W. Scotland; site of remains of a castle and a cathedral.)
7. Seekonk? (Navigable river about 5 miles long in N.E. Rhode Island.)
8. Valera? (Town in Venezuela.)
9. Halland? (Province of Sweden.)
10. Austronesia? (In general, the islands of the South Pacific Ocean; more accurately, the vast island area.)
11. Amager? (Island forming a part of Denmark.)
12. Loja? (Province of Ecuador.)
13. Charing Cross? (District in London, England.)
14. Niger? (River about 2600 miles long in West Africa.)
15. Shensi? (Province in N.E. Central China.)
16. Nakskov? (Seaport in Denmark.)
17. Farmington? (A river in northern Connecticut.)
18. Grays Peak? (A mountain 14,274 ft. in Clear Creek

and Summit Os., central Colorado; highest peak in the
Front Range.)
19. Biscay? (A province of Spain.)
20. Bintan? (An island, the largest of the Riouw Archi-
pelago, Indonesia, off southern tip of the Malay Penin-
sula.)

141. Van Nostrand's Scientific Encyclopedia

What are the following, using *Van Nostrand's Scientific Encyclopedia*? (D. Van Nostrand Co., 1958.)

1. Binnacle? (The stand for supporting and protecting
the compass on board a ship.)
2. Gusts? (Transient but rapid fluctuations of wind velocity. Gusts are the result of turbulent air flow. Gusty
winds usually vary radically in direction.)
3. Vug? (A rock cavity lined, but incompletely filled,
with mineral matter so that a part of the available
spore remains empty.)
4. Mesa? (A flat-topped, steep-sided, tablelike mountain capped with a formation or stratum which is rela-
tively horizontal and resistant to erosion.)
5. Radio Astronomy? (The basis of radio astronomy is
the fact that various stars, planets, nebulae and other
bodies and regions of the universe are the source of
radio waves.)
6. Stark effect? (The effect of a strong, transverse electric field upon the spectrum lines of a gas subjected to
its influence.)
7. Nemertea? (Class of marine worms with a flattened
body, often long and ribbonlike in form.)
8. Carbonado? (Black diamond: the mineral carbonado is an opaque, massive, black variety of diamond.)
9. Flower pecker? (Brightly colored birds [Aves] of the
Oriental and Australian regions, related to the sun
birds and having remarkable nests.)
10. Intussusception? (The telescoping of one section of

the intestine into the part below, causing intestinal obstruction; caused by neuromuscular incoordination.)

11. Shooting star? (Popular term used to designate meteors. These objects bear little if any relation to the stars other than that they are seen as bright, rapidly moving objects against the dark sky and hence apparently among the stars.)

12. Throwing power? (A term used to denote the relative effectiveness of various electrolytic cells for the deposition of metal at the cathode.)

13. Devonian? (The name of a geologic period.)

14. Epithelium? (Tissue which covers surfaces and lines hollow organs, and the derivatives of these tissues, whether solid or hollow.)

15. Relativity Theory, Special? (Theory developed by Einstein based on the hypothesis that the velocity of light is the same as measured by any one of a set of observers moving with constant relative velocity.)

16. Shadow Zone? (A region, usually in the atmosphere or under water, in which ray acoustics predicts zero penetration of sound rays.)

17. Guttation? (The loss of liquid water from intact plants.)

18. Radio Telegraphy? (That form of radio communication which utilizes the dots and dashes of the International code to transmit intelligence.)

19. Ammeter? (An instrument for measuring electric currents in amperes.)

20. Convection currents? (Air currents that travel vertically.)

142. Famous First Facts

Using *Famous First Facts* (Joseph Nathan Kane; H.W. Wilson Co., 1964), who, what, or when was the first . . .?

1. Congressman of Japanese ancestry elected to the House of Representatives? (David Ken Inouye.)

2. Vice president to marry in office? (Alben William Barkley.)

3. Circulating library? (Library Company of Philadelphia in 1732.)

4. Anesthesia used? (In 1842, a general anesthetic operation performed — C.W. Long in Jefferson, Ga.)

5. White House wedding? (In 1812, Justice Thomas Todd.)

6. State hospital for the insane? (In 1773, in Williamsburg, Va.)

7. World Series Baseball Game to gross a million dollars? (1923 in New York City.)

8. Juvenile court cases tried by a woman judge? (1913, in Chicago, Ill.)

9. Siamese twins brought to Boston, Mass.? (On August 16, 1829 — Chang and Eng [Bunker]. Born on April 15, 1811.)

10. Airmail service? (In 1946 — helicopter airmail delivery in Bridgeport, Conn., on July 5th.)

11. Radar signal to the moon? (1946 — Belmar, N.J., on Jan. 10th.)

12. Sewing machine to stitch buttonholes? (Patented by Charles Miller on March 7, 1854.)

13. Woman army officer? (Mary A. Hallaren, sworn in Dec. 3, 1948.)

14. Round-the-world telephone conversation? (April 25, 1935, in New York City.)

15. 200-inch telescope lens used? (Feb. 1, 1949.)

16. Atomic bomb — underground explosion? (Nov. 29, 1951, in Frenchman Flat, Nev.)

17. American orchestra to make a European tour? (May 4, 1920 — concert in Paris, France.)

18. Snow-melting apparatus with pipe imbedded in the sidewalk used? (Tested on Dec. 8, 1946, and in actual operation during a blizzard on Dec. 26, 1946.)

19. Supreme court decision establishing the power of the United States as greater than that of the individual state? (Made Feb. 20, 1809.)

20. Commercial fishery established? (1629 in Medford, Mass.)

143. Webster's
Biographical Dictionary

Using *Webster's Biographical Dictionary* (G. & C. Merriam Co.), who were the following people, and when did they live?

1. Wanda Gag? (American painter, author, and illustrator: 1893–1946.)
2. Ralph Mershon? (American electrical engineer and inventor; inventor of 6-place rotary converter: 1868–1952.)
3. William Tudor? (American author: 1779–1830; founder and first editor, *North American Review*.)
4. Francesco Carrara? (Italian jurist; instructor in criminal law: 1805–1888.)
5. Stewart Balfour? (Scottish physicist and meteorologist: 1828–1887.)
6. Mary Garden? (Operatic soprano: 1874–1967.)
7. John Carroll? (American Roman Catholic prelate: 1735–1815.)
8. William Thomas Sampson? (American naval officer: 1840–1902.)
9. Sancho Ramirez? (Son of Ramiro I of Aragon and grandson of Sancho the Great; king (1076–94) who fought Moorish kings of Saragossa & Huesca.)
10. Lysias? (162 B.C. Syrian general & regent under kings Antiochus Epiphanes & Antiochus Eupator. Appointed viceroy 165 B.C.)
11. Chauncey Tinker? (American educator; teacher of English, Yale University, from 1903, and professor from 1913; authority on Dr. Samuel Johnson and his period in English; 1876–1963.)
12. George Pullman? (American inventor; cabinetmaker in Albion, N.Y.; designed Pullman car with folding upper berth and extensible seat cushions to make lower berth. Designed dining cars, chair cars and vestibule cars: 1831–1897.)
13. George Eastman? (American inventor and industrialist; perfected process for making photographic dry

plates in 1880 and flexible film in 1884; invented the Kodak in 1888: 1854–1932.)

14. Ernest Lawrence? (American physicist; invented the cyclotron, by means of which he researched the structure of the atom, effected transmutation of certain elements, and produced artificial radioactivity; 1901–1958.)

15. Oldenburg? (A German family of nobility which became prominent in the fifteenth century; it is divided into several lines.)

144. Men of Science

Using the *McGraw-Hill Modern Men of Science* (the editors of *McGraw-Hill Encyclopedia of Science & Technology*, 1966), who were the following men of science?

1. Othmar Hermann Ammann? (American engineer; designed Lincoln tunnel.)

2. Curt Stern? (Made contributions in a variety of areas of general and human genetics; determined that recombination of genes linked together on same chromosome pair is result of chromosome exchanges.)

3. Donald Arthur Glaser? (Invented the "bubble chamber," a device for detecting the paths of high energy atomic particles.)

4. Sir Harold (Spencer) Jones? (Directed the redetermination of the value of the astronomical unit, the mean distance between the sun and earth.)

5. Max Theiler? (Developed a vaccine that prevented human yellow fever infection.)

6. George Deacon? (Went to Antarctica to improve our understanding of migrations, variations in distribution, and fluctuations in populations of the Antarctic winds.)

7. Bengt Stromgren? (Studied gaseous nebulae, the interstellar, sometimes luminous clouds occurring thoughout galaxy; concluded that luminous regions must consist of hydrogen, ionized by radiation.)

8. John Foster, Jr.? (Made contributions in application

of nuclear explosives to military and peaceful uses. Best known for a breakthrough in small or tactical nuclear weapons.)

9. Archibald Huntsman? (Solved a problem with which fishermen must deal: what fish will be where, and when? This question typifies the general problem of what life there will be at any particular time & place.)

10. Britton Chance? (Interested in the measurement of rapid reactions in solutions, he perfected before World War II new types of flow methods employing oscillographic readout which he termed "stopped flow method" and "accelerated flow method.")

11. Thomas Weller? (Isolated the viruses of chicken pox and shingles and proved the common etiology of these two diseases.)

12. Edwin Land? (Made contributions in fields of polarized light, photography, and color vision.)

13. Edmund Ford? (Made contributions to the genetical theory of evolution by natural selection, particularly in natural populations.)

14. Henry Taube? (Principal contributions were in the area of inorganic reactions in solution.)

15. John KenDrew? (Made first successful determination of the structure of a protein.)

16. William Shockley? (Discovered the transistor effect for electronic amplification by means of solid-state semiconductors, which were smaller, less fragile, and more efficient.)

17. Arthur Holmes? (Puzzled and fascinated by date 400 B.C., traditionally assigned to creation of world as described in Bible; plotted radiometric dates.)

18. Daniel Bovet? (Observed organic compounds that proved effective as muscle relaxants, used to supplement light general anesthesia during surgery, and as antihistamines useful in alleviating effects of allergies.)

19. Feodor Lynen? (Made discoveries concerning mechanisms and regulation of cholesterol and fatty acid metabolism.)

20. Merle Tuve? (Had great skill in applying electronics to almost any given problem.)

21. Jerome Hunsaker? (Measured the force on a turning destroyer's rudder, which led to estimation of the aerodynamic forces on airplanes by model tests in a wind tunnel.)
22. Ernest Lawrence? (Inventor of the cyclotron.)
23. Sir James Chadwick? (Established experimentally the existence of the neutron-a particle, whose presence in atomic nuclei he had suspected since 1920.)
24. Chauncey Suits? (Added to man's knowledge of what takes place within an electric arc.)
25. Sir Bernard Lovell? (Proved the applicability of radar studies to meteor showers using ex-military radar apparatus immediately after World War II.)

145. Great Composers

Name at least one piece of music that the following composers composed, using *Great Composers 1300–1900* (David Ewen; The H.W. Wilson Co., 1966) and *Composers Since 1900* (David Ewen; The H.W. Wilson Co., 1969).

1. Bedrich Smetana? (Example: *choral*, "Sea Song"; *vocal*, "Evening Songs.")
2. Edvard Grieg? (Example: *orchestral*, "Norwegian Dances"; "In Autumn.")
3. William Byrd? (Example: *choral*, "My Little Sweet Darling"; over 250 motets.)
4. Alexander Scriabin? (Example: *orchestral*, "The Poem of Ecstasy.")
5. Igor Stravinsky? (Example: *ballet*, "The Firebird.")
6. Franz Liszt? (Example: *piano music*, 19 Hungarian Rhapsodies.)
7. Richard Wagner? (Example: "Der Ring des Nibelungen.")
8. Felix Mendelssohn? (Example: *orchestral*, "A Midsummer Night's Dream.")
9. Claude Debussy? (Example: *orchestral*, "Prelude a l'Apres Midi d'un Faune.")
10. Joseph Haydn? (Example: *choral*, "The Creation.")

11. Aram Khatchaturian? (Example: *ballet*, "Happiness.")
12. Sergei Prokofiev? (Example: *ballet*, "L'Enfant Prodigue.")
13. Georges Bizet? (Example: *orchestral*, "Petite Suite.")
14. Ludwig Van Beethoven? (Example: 9 symphonies; bagatelles.)
15. Manuel de Falla? (Example: *orchestral*, "Nights in the Gardens of Spain.")
16. Antonio Vivaldi? (Example: *vocal*, "Stabat Mater.")
17. Johann Sebastian Bach? (Example: *clavier*: "The Art of the Fugue.")
18. Erik Satie? (Example: *piano*, "Gymnopédies.")
19. Frederic Chopin? (Example: 55 mazurkas; "Barcarolle in F-sharp minor.")
20. Anton Bruckner? (Example: *piano*, "Klavierstück in E-flat major.")
21. Charles Ives? (Example: *orchestral*, "Central Park in the Dark.")
22. George Gershwin? (Example: *orchestral*, "Rhapsody in Blue.")
23. Richard Strauss? (Example: *chamber*, "Metamorphosen.")
24. Aaron Copland? (Example: *ballet*, "Appalachian Spring.")
25. Gustav Mahler? (Example: *orchestral*, "Das Klagende Lied.")

146. Junior Book of Authors

Using the "Junior Author Series" — *The Junior Book of Authors* (Kunitz and Haycraft; H.W. Wilson Co., 1951); *More Junior Authors* (Fuller; H.W. Wilson Co., 1963); *Third Book of Junior Authors* (De Montreville and Hill; H.W. Wilson Co., 1972); *Fourth Book of Junior Authors and Illustrators* (De Montreville and Crawford; H.W. Wilson Co., 1978) — (A) name one novel written; and (B) tell one interesting fact about the following authors (answers given below are examples):

1. Eleanor Cameron. (A) *The wonderful flight to the*

mushroom planet; (B) Was a librarian.
2. Walter Farley. (A) *The Black Stallion*; (B) Breeds and raises horses.
3. Robert Heinlein. (A) *Time for the Stars*; (B) Has a hobby of astronomy.
4. Frank Bonham. (A) *Durango Street*; (B) Also writes books about dolphins and submarines, jungle warfare, and life in Baja, Calif.
5. Judy Blume. (A) *Are You There God? It's Me, Margaret*; (B) She likes to write about feelings.
6. S.E. Hinton. (A) *The Outsiders*; (B) Her name is Susan Eloise Hinton Inhofe; she made a D in creative writing when she was a junior in high school.
7. Paul-Jacques Bonzon. (A) *The Orphans of Simitra*; (B) Favorite themes are comradeship, friendship and devotion.
8. *Virginia Hamilton. (A) M.C. Higgins the Great*; (B) Her greatest pleasure is weaving a tale out of the mystery of her past and present.
9. Marilyn Sachs. (A) *Veronica Ganz*; (B) Worked as a children's librarian with the Brooklyn Public Library for 10 years.
10. Lester Del Rey. (A) *Marooned on Mars*; (B) His first story was written on a dare from a friend.
11. Emily Neville. (A) *It's Like This, Cat*; (B) She was 10 years old before she went to public school.
12. Maia Wojciechowska. (A) *Shadow of a Bull*; (B) She says to be the best you can be, and the rest will take care of itself.
13. Donald Sobol. (A) *Encyclopedia Brown*; (B) In the 1960s he wrote the nationally syndicated newspaper feature "Two Minute Mystery Series."
14. Kate Seredy. (A) *The White Stag*; (B) Author and illustrator.
15. Elizabeth Yates. (A) *Patterns on the Wall*; (B) Lived in London and traveled; reading is her joy.
16. Sylvia Louise Engdahl. (A) *Enchantress from the Stars*; (B) Has a deep interest in space travel.
17. Robert Lawson. (A) *Rabbit Hill*; (B) He built a house in Westport, Conn., called "Rabbit Hill."
18. Laura Ingalls Wilder. (A) *The Little House in the Big*

Woods; (B) The truth she learned from parents and the principles taught by them are always true and can never change.

19. Jules Verne. (A) *Twenty Thousand Leagues Under the Sea*; (B) Wrote over 100 books, and they have been translated into practically every language.

20. Paula Fox. (A) *The Slave Dancer*; (B) She discovered that freedom, solace and truth were in the public libraries.

147. Music Search

Find the following information using the reference section of the library:

1. With whom did George Gershwin take piano lessons? (Charles Hambitzer.) *Biographical Dictionary of American Music*, p. 169 (Charles E. Claghorn; Parker Pub., 1973).

2. What happened when Prokofiev was asked to write an opera and he composed "The Gambler"? (It was found unsingable and unplayable.) *Composers Since 1900*, p. 432 (David Ewen; H.W. Wilson, 1969).

3. What composer was Maurice Ravel accused of plagiarizing? (Debussy.) *The New Music Lover's Handbook*, p. 281 (ed. by Elie Siegmeister; Harvey House, 1973).

4. When was "The Marriage of Figaro" by Mozart introduced? (May 1, 1786.) *Great Composers 1300–1900*, p. 265 (David Ewen; H.W. Wilson, 1966).

5. Name one characteristic of the Romantic Movement in music. (Making music poetical and picturesque, and poetry musical.) *The New Music Lover's Handbook*, p. 191 (ed. by Elie Siegmeister; Harvey House, 1973).

6. What was Manuel DeFalla's music credo? ("Our music must be based on the natural music of our people, on the dances and songs, that do not always show close kinship.") *Composers Since 1900*, p. 193 (David Ewen; H.W. Wilson, 1969).

7. When did oratorio originate? (Not until after 1600.)

The New Music Lover's Handbook, p. 111 (ed. by Elie Siegmeister; Harvey House, 1973).

8. What instruments provided accompaniment for the earliest films? (Pianos and harmoniums.) *The New Music Lover's Handbook*, p. 332 (ed. by Elie Siegmeister; Harvey House, 1973).

9. What are the dates of Baroque music? (1600–1750.) *The New Music Lover's Handbook*, p. 129 (ed. by Elie Siegmeister; Harvey House, 1973).

10. In the modern orchestra, how many strings are employed? (About 65.) *The New Music Lover's Handbook*, p. 74 (ed. by Elie Siegmeister; Harvey House, 1973).

148. Historical Word Search

Using the *Dictionary of American Biography* (Charles Scribner's, 1961), find the answers to these questions and circle them on the puzzle (they appear across, diagonally, and vertically):

1. Bicycling became popular in late 1860s. Who imported bicycles from England and later manufactured them? (Albert A. Pope.)
2. Ohio's Big Bottom Massacre was by which Indians? (Shawnee.)
3. Another name for campaign song? (Partisan ditty.)
4. A farm machine that makes harvesting and threshing a single process? (Combine.)
5. Aleutian Islands discovered by–? (Vitus Bering.)
6. This act established an 8-hour day instead of 10 for the railroad trainmen. (Adamson Act.)
7. The United States Army is modeled primarily upon that of which other country? (England.)
8. The modern campaign slogan dated from 1840, with its famous slogan "_____ and Tyler too." (Tippecanoe.)
9. The first colonial newspaper published in Boston in 1690 was–? (*Publick Occurences.*)
10. Who wrote the tract "Common Sense," published in Philadelphia? (Thomas Paine.)

```
A  D  A  M  S  O  N  A  C  T  E  M  E
J  L  B  C  D  E  F  H  G  I  J  O  I
B  N  B  E  R  I  N  G  M  L  N  K  T
E  O  P  E  Q  R  W  V  U  A  T  S  E
A  B  T  C  R  A  S  D  C  U  F  W  N
N  Z  F  R  G  T  Y  E  X  H  V  R  I
E  A  A  D  B  F  P  U  B  L  I  C  K
K  E  P  I  I  P  E  O  T  L  B  I  E
A  L  O  T  I  E  A  S  P  E  E  A  E
L  X  Y  T  E  I  Z  I  J  E  T  E  H
T  I  O  Y  I  D  E  O  N  I  E  E  D
A  R  L  C  O  M  B  I  N  E  M  N  A
E  N  D  E  J  G  K  E  N  N  O  E  E
S  Q  E  A  K  O  N  W  I  G  J  U  G
I  M  H  F  C  V  A  C  E  L  O  N  P
O  R  S  M  A  H  I  G  P  I  U  E  E
O  L  H  M  S  U  N  N  O  S  P  L  O
S  I  A  N  O  N  T  M  S  H  I  O  L
```

149. Science Word Scramble

Find the following answers within the scrambled words using
A Dictionary of Scientific Terms (Foundations of Science Library,
1966):

1. A small space within the protoplasm of a cell.
   LEVOACU (vacuole.)
2. An animal which eats other animals. NEACROVIR
   (carnivore.)
3. Branch of science which deals with the measurement
   of heat. MACITYOELRR (calorimetry.)

4. Leaf-like outgrowth at base of leaf-stalk. PITESUL (stipule.)
5. Junction between nerve cells. PYNSAES (synapse.)
6. Outermost parts of every atom. LOEENTCRS (electrons.)
7. A type of inflorescence — for example, bluebells with stalked flowers on a main axis. CAREEM (raceme.)
8. The association of two different organisms in which both receive advantages. BYOSIMISS (symbiosis.)
9. A plant which completes its life cycle in one year. NAUALN (annual.)
10. Primitive flowerless plants. GALEA (algae.)

150. Reference Relay

How good are your research skills? Working with your group, you will have ____ minutes in order to look up the answers to as many of the following ten questions as you can. Record not only the answers but also the name of your sources and the page upon which you found your answer. The group that finishes first is the winner!

1. Kent Island is how many miles long? What is it?
   a. Answer:
   b. Source:
   c. Page:
2. Who is Georgette Heyer?
   a. Answer:
   b. Source:
   c. Page:
3. When is the harvest moon? The moon moves eastward among the stars in an orbit inclined at how many degrees?
   a. Answer:
   b. Source:
   c. Page:
4. When was the first transatlantic helicopter flight made?
   a. Answer:
   b. Source:
   c. Page:

5. What is a synonym for gelid?
   a. Answer:
   b. Source:
   c. Page:
6. What are the various types of grafts in plastic surgery?
   a. Answer:
   b. Source:
   c. Page:
7. In folklore, what does the motif of the "grateful dead" mean?
   a. Answer:
   b. Source:
   c. Page:
8. What is the old meaning of the word "today"?
   a. Answer:
   b. Source:
   c. Page:
9. How many gates did Jean-Claude Killy plunge through on the 1,040 meter course?
   a. Answer:
   b. Source:
   c. Page:
10. Who was Gazaway Bugg Lamar?
    a. Answer:
    b. Source:
    c. Page:

151. Reference Tools

The class is divided into 3 teams. Of the reference books found in the library, each team must list at least 2 titles of each of the following categories of reference sources: bibliographies, indexes and abstracts, encyclopedias, subject encyclopedias, dictionaries, quotations, almanacs, special subject almanacs, yearbooks/annuals, directories, handbooks and manuals, biographical sources, geographical sources, statistical reference sources, and government documents. The first team to list 2 titles within each category is the winner.

152. Lexicon Label

Using all kinds of dictionaries in your library, in which would you find the following terms?

1. protocol, whitewash, town board? *Dictionary of American Politics* (McCarthy; Macmillan, 1968).
2. firebreak, field test, lentic? *Dictionary of Ecology* (Philosophical Library, 1962).
3. internal conversion? *Van Nostrand's Scientific Encyclopedia* (D. Van Nostrand Co., 1958).
4. nasturtium, compunction? *Dictionary of Word and Phrase Origins* (William & Mary Morris; Harper & Row, 1967).
5. melodious, quandary? *The Doubleday Roget's Thesaurus in Dictionary Form* (Landau, *et al.*; Doubleday, 1977).
6. sag, fence-off, feint? *Webster's Sports Dictionary* (G. & C. Merriam Co., 1976).
7. Guanal Point, Ashley? *Webster's Geographical Dictionary* (G. & C. Merriam Co., 1967).
8. William Lauder? *Webster's Biographical Dictionary* (G. & C. Merriam Co., 1966).
9. Battle of Guilford Court House? *A Dictionary of Battles* (Eggenberger; Crowell, 1967).
10. What word rhymes with sand? *The Complete Rhyming Dictionary* (ed. by Wood; Doubleday, 1936).

153. Wealth of Resources

Students may do this one individually, or the class may be divided into two teams. Below are ten questions followed by a list of ten reference books in which you would look for the answers. Match the proper book to each question and write the letter A–J next to that question.

    <u>E</u>   1. A world-famous quotation by Muhammed Ali?
    <u>G</u>   2. A simple definition followed by a more detailed technical explanation of a subject in energy technology?

D   3. A political and historical map of France?

B   4. Profiles on art exhibitions and museums in the U.S.?

J   5. Statistics and facts on a political subject?

H   6. An article and a photograph of author Jack Ezra Keats?

C   7. The birthdate of Paul Newman?

A   8. The pH of the water that all fishes will generally do well in?

I   9. The meaning of "major foul" in the sport of water polo?

P   10. Current information on cancer research?

A. *Breeding Aquarium Fishes* (Axelrod. T.F.H., 1976).

B. *American Art Directory* (ed. by Jacques Cattell Press; Bowker, 1980).

C. *World Almanac and Book of Facts* (Newspaper Enterprise Assoc., 1980).

D. *Hammond Medallion World Atlas* (Hammond, 1977).

E. *Bartlett's Familiar Quotations* (Bartlett, Little, Brown & Co., 1955).

F. *Abridged Readers' Guide* (H.W. Wilson Co.).

G. *Van Nostrand's Scientific Encyclopedia* (D. Van Nostrand, 1958).

H. *More Junior Authors* (Fuller. H.W. Wilson Co., 1963).

I. *Webster's Sports Dictionary* (G. & C. Merriam-Webster, 1976).

J. *Statesman's Yearbook* (ed. by Paxton; Macmillan, 1970).

154. Trivia Subject Pursuit

For each subject of the curriculum, the library media specialist may devise a group of questions for a trivia pursuit game. Interesting trivia may be collected from the latest *Guinness Book of World Records* (Norris McWhirter; Sterling, 1985), or use any of the other reference sources in the library.

Part VI
Quiet Mental Games

155. Worldly-Wise

1. What country is warm to snuggle up to? (Afghanistan.)
2. What country is full of frozen water? (Iceland.)
3. What country is a hot spicy food? (Chile.)
4. What country is good to eat on Thanksgiving? (Turkey.)
5. What country suggests a particular kind of hat? (Panama.)
6. What country is also the name of a chain store? (Zaire [Zayre].)
7. What country helps fish to move? (Finland.)
8. What country suggests a cigar? (Cuba.)
9. What country is also a nut? (Brazil.)
10. What country is very together? (United States.)
11. What country do you oil the squeaky door with? (Greece.)
12. What country makes you gain weight? (Hungary.)
13. What country is also special dishware? (China.)
14. What country is also a boy's name? (Chad.)
15. What country is also a boy's or girl's name? (Jordan.)

156. Summary

You need to know your Roman numerals for this one!

1. 50 plus a huge boat = a bird. (Lark.)
2. 5 plus a type of beer = a headpiece. (Veil.)
3. 1,000 plus you hurt = ? (Make.)
4. 500 plus the 12th letter of the alphabet = ? (Dell.)
5. 5 plus a girl's name = ? (Van.)
6. 1,000 plus everything = a shopping plaza. (Mall.)
7. 500 plus either . . . = ? (Door.)
8. 1,000 plus the first letter of the alphabet = ? (May.)
9. 50 plus singular of verb to be = ? (Lamb.)
10. 5 plus ace = ? (Vase.)
11. 500 plus a large boat = without light? (Dark.)
12. 5 plus the scotch for own = a weather? (Vane.)

157. Mishmash

This game may be used in history, science, math, English, music, art or any other class. Make up a chart with various topics listed vertically in the left-hand column. Across the top, spell out the name of the subject, making one column under each letter. Students must fill in an appropriate term beginning with the correct letter in each column, as on the sample chart below.

Categories	M	U	S	I	C
Composer	Mozart	Ussachevsky	Schönberg	Ives	Copland
Instrument	Mandolin	Ukulele	Saxophone	Idiophones	Cello
Musical Composition					
Musical Term	Moderato	Una Corda	Sostenuto	Internal	Crescendo

Students may be divided into groups, or they may work on this activity individually in their own time. The idea is to fill up all the categories if possible. The group or individual who finishes with the most correct fill-ins wins. Students may jot down more than one word for each category for extra points.

158. 3-D Tic-Tac-Toe

Draw a cube, represented by 48 squares, as shown below. Four answers in a row is the winner: horizontally, vertically or diagonally.

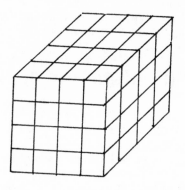

Instead of writing in X's or O's, students can write authors, titles, or characters from fiction. Categories such as animal characters, fantasy characters, for instance, may be selected as the X's and science fiction or historical fiction as the O's.

159. Word for Word

This activity may be modified for play by a few students or by the entire class.

Each student draws a square divided into four squares across by four squares down, sixteen squares in all. The librarian calls out a letter of the alphabet. Each student jots the letter down in any square of his choosing. The librarian calls out a second letter, and again, each student jots the letter down in any square. The object is to write the letters down as they are called, in such a way that they will spell words of at least two letters, reading either across or down. Letters cannot be moved to another box once they have been written down.

Depending on which class is visiting, words written down can be relevant to the subject matter. However, if the social studies or science class is visiting the library, the number of squares can be increased (say, seven by seven) to allow for longer words.

The librarian continues to call out letters until students have filled as many boxes as possible. The number of points is equal to the amount of letters used in each term. In addition, if a word fills all the squares in a row, one bonus point may be awarded. The ending of a word may not form the beginning of another word in the same row. Each student adds together all his horizontal and vertical totals, the winner being the one with the highest score.

160. Metamorphosis

This is another word game suitable for English, science, math or any other subject classes. Two words having an equal number of letters are selected. Each student writes down the two words. He attempts to change the first word into the second word by altering only one letter at a time, and each time forming a new word. With the science class, for example, change "till" to "tide" (till — tile — tide). The winner is the student who makes the transformation using the least number of words.

161. Fill-In Fun

This activity may be correlated to any subject of the curriculum. A list of 10–20 words is given. Each student is then given the first and last letters, and the number of letters missing, from each word on the list. A time limit is set. The winner is the student who has the most correct words.

For example, here is a list of names and places corresponding to the Middle East:

1. B _ _ _ _ _ D (Baghdad.)
2. H _ _ _ _ _ N (Hussein.)
3. O _ L (Oil.)
4. E _ _ N (Eban.)
5. E _ _ _ T (Egypt.)
6. M _ _ R (Meir.)
7. I _ _ Q (Iraq.)

8. P _ _ _ _ _ I (Pahlevi.)
9. L _ _ _ _ A (Libya.)
10. S _ _ _ T (Sadat.)

162. Logical Thinking

What is "logical" in:

1. families and ancestors? (genealogical.)
2. rocks? (geological.)
3. life? (biological.)
4. the sky? (cosmological.)
5. animals? (zoological.)
6. the mind? (psychological.)
7. the weather? (meteorological.)
8. time? (chronological.)
9. science? (technological.)

163. Beastly Blooms

Name the flowering plants that are also names of animals.

1. enormous eater of nuisance plants? (pigweed.)
2. a purring bite? (catnip.)
3. a rooster's hair instrument? (cockscomb.)
4. a trunked hearer? (elephant's-ear.)
5. a smelly vegetable? (skunk cabbage.)
6. a feather of bliss? (Bird-of-paradise.)
7. a slithering reptile anchored underground? (snake-root.)
8. the mature female of cattle that slides? (cowslip.)
9. a feline's appendage? (cattail.)
10. an adult female swine with thorns? (sow thistle.)
11. a bird that stimulates? (larkspur.)
12. a pet poison? (dogbane.)
13. abrupt seizing dinosaur? (snapdragon.)
14. a male deer that pricks? (buckthorn.)
15. naked and creeping xylem? (wormwood.)
16. frog linen? (toadflax.)

17. a mischievous primate blossom? (monkey flower.)
18. a clever, crafty mitt? (foxglove.)
19. a carnivorous funnel-shaped flower? (tiger lily.)
20. a galloping pungent fleshy root? (horseradish.)

164. Posy Probe

What flower:

1. is part of the eye? (iris.)
2. scrambled is "saliva"? (salvia.)
3. is a purplish-red? (fuchsia.)
4. does what frogs do? (crocus.)
5. is part of a fish? (delphinium.)
6. rings true blue? (bluebells of Scotland.)
7. contains part of the face? (tulip.)
8. are girls with dark eyes? (black-eyed Susans.)
9. wears a hat? (bluebonnet.)
10. comes out of the sky? (shooting star.)
11. wears a lady's clothing? (pink lady's-slipper.)
12. is a little yellow? (dwarf marigold.)
13. encompasses a country? (carnation.)
14. is easy to remember? (forget-me-not.)
15. contains a food flavoring? (daffodil.)
16. acts as a pillar? (columbine.)
17. is part of the foot? (mistletoe.)
18. worships the sun? (sunflower.)
19. is a springtime fruit? (may apple.)
20. encompasses the world? (cosmos.)

165. Special Delivery

What postal abbreviations could be matched to the following?

1. myself? (ME — Maine.)
2. a boy's name? (AL — Alabama.)
3. a nickname for mother? (MA — Massachusetts.)
4. opposite of out? (IN — Indiana.)

5. a doctor? (MD — Maryland.)
6. an exclamation? (OH — Ohio.)
7. an alternative? (OR — Oregon.)
8. acceptable? (OK — Oklahoma.)
9. hello? (HI — Hawaii.)
10. meaning public relations? (PR — Puerto Rico.)
11. a veteran's organization? (VA — Virginia.)
12. with or together? (CO — Colorado.)

166. Meter Measure

Give a word that ends in "meter" and sounds like:

1. Your measurements determine your clothing ...? (seismometer.)
2. prefix meaning time? (chronometer.)
3. drinks at a ...? (barometer.)
4. tenor, bass, soprano ...? (altometer.)
5. tacky? (tachometer.)
6. wash in a ...? (bathometer.)
7. to go fast? (speedometer.)
8. What causes lightning? (electrometer.)
9. a guy and a ...? (galvanometer.)
10. prefix meaning hearing? (audiometer.)
11. Latin for "sound"? (sonometer.)
12. The colors of the rainbow? (spectrometer.)
13. a layer of the atmosphere? (stratometer.)
14. rhymes with no go? (logometer.)

167. Phony Baloney

Give a word that ends with "phony" or "phany" and sounds like:

1. what a crow says? (cacophony.)
2. prefix meaning same? (homophony.)
3. prefix meaning small? (microphony.)
4. vocal cords? (laryngophony.)

5. prefix meaning straightening or corrective? (ortho-phony.)
6. a picture? (photophony.)
7. devil? (satanophany.)
8. Dorothy's dog? (tautophony.)
9. Kojak's first name? (theophany.)

168. Analyze Your Ability

Give a word that ends with "ability" and sounds like:

1. to change? (modifiability, mutability.)
2. measure? (mensurability.)
3. not to tell the truth? (liability.)
4. prominent? (notability.)
5. logical, useful? (practicability.)
6. bendable? (pliability.)
7. to take away? (removability.)
8. not permitting passage? (impermeability.)
9. stationary? (immovability.)
10. strong and long-lasting? (durability.)
11. believable? (credibility.)
12. worthy of praise? (admirability, laudability.)
13. competent? (capability.)
14. accessible? (availability.)
15. able to be handled? (manageability.)
16. holding steady? (stability.)
17. best choice? (preferability.)
18. easily moved? (portability.)

169. Mineralogy

What mineral:

1. has the same name as its coin? (nickel.)
2. helps preserve leftover food? (aluminum.)
3. is used in a thermometer? (mercury.)
4. makes a beautiful necklace? (silver.)
5. is food packaged in? (tin.)

6. is used as fireproof material? (asbestos.)
7. was used in paint? (lead.)
8. is therapy for illness? (cobalt.)
9. can smooth out wrinkles? (iron.)
10. is blonder than blonde? (platinum.)

170. Ferous Furnish

Give a word that ends with "ferous":

1. petrified remains? (fossiliferous.)
2. charcoal? (carboniferous.)
3. engagement stone? (diamondiferous.)
4. flower? (floriferous.)
5. gas? (vaporiferous.)
6. a coin? (nickeliferous.)
7. smell? (odoriferous.)
8. flavoring? (herbiferous.)
9. a Romanian living a migrant life? (gypsiferous.)
10. a root you plant in the spring? (bulbiferous.)
11. a substance that eats away? (acidiferous.)
12. a fleshy root? (tuberiferous.)

171. Flaunt the Flag

Have library aides construct flags out of construction paper or oak tag. Students may match the country with the flag. Consult *World Almanac* (Newspaper Enterprise Assoc.) or another reference source.

172. Cake Bazaar

What kind of cake sounds like:

1. a cooking utensil? (pancake.)
2. one who has wings and wears a halo? (angelcake.)
3. a centerpiece for the dining room table? (fruitcake.)
4. a beverage in the morning? (coffeecake.)

5. to drink from a ...? (cupcake.)
6. a measurement? (pound cake.)
7. something that adds flavor? (spice cake.)
8. something that soaks up spills? (sponge cake.)
9. a dairy product? (cheese cake.)
10. geologic folds? (layer cake.)
11. a liquor? (rum cake.)

173. Snake in the Grass

What is the name of a snake that:

1. is a president or a ruler? (king.)
2. is a wet shoe? (water moccasin.)
3. is a baby's toy? (rattle.)
4. is an undersea jewel? (coral.)
5. is a white liquid? (milk.)
6. is lingerie? (garter.)
7. is dark? (black.)
8. is a shrub leader? (bushmaster.)
9. is an orange top? (copperhead.)
10. rhymes with ladder? (adder.)
11. is a male of a bovine animal? (bullsnake.)
12. is a ground squirrel? (gopher.)
13. is a pig snout? (hognose.)
14. is a long-tailed rodent? (rat snake.)
15. is a cunning person? (fox snake.)
16. is a skin blemish? (mole snake.)
17. is maize? (corn snake.)
18. is an arc of colors? (rainbow snake.)
19. is wet, soft earth? (mud snake.)

174. Wangling Worms

What kind of worm sounds like:

1. a curved fastener? (hookworm.)
2. a planet? (earthworm.)
3. a narrow strip? (ribbon worm.)

4. circular? (roundworm.)
5. snakelike fish? (eelworm.)
6. a straight fastener? (pinworm.)
7. 2-dimensional? (flatworm.)
8. a sticky narrow strip? (tapeworm.)
9. part of an ear? (lobworm.)
10. old paper? (parchment worm.)
11. granular rocks? (sandworm.)

175. Animal By-Products

Name the animal by-product:

1. Used for sweetening? (honey.)
2. Used for sticking things together? (glue.)
3. that makes beautiful sweaters? (cashmere.)
4. that is an oyster jewel? (pearl.)
5. that smells nice? (perfume.)
6. that protects cars and furniture? (wax.)
7. that makes warm clothing? (wool.)
8. that makes an itchy sweater? (mohair.)
9. that is needed by people with diabetes? (insulin.)
10. that makes soft and luxurious clothing? (silk.)
11. that gives you smooth hands? (lanolin.)
12. that is used on piano keys? (ivory.)
13. that is a breakfast food? (egg.)
14. that is a dessert? (gelatin.)

176. Lily Lore

What kind of lily (flower) sounds like:

1. an Asian's hat? (Turk's-cap lily.)
2. jaundiced water? (yellow pond lily.)
3. a forgetful fruit? (lotus-lily.)
4. something wet? (water lily.)
5. an undomesticated pungent herb? (wild onion.)
6. crimson + 3 + small intestine? (red trillium.)
7. a clean plant? (soapweed.)

8. xylem? (wood lily.)
9. opposite of night? (day lily.)
10. our northern neighbor? (Canada lily.)
11. between 2 hills or mountains? (lily-of-the-valley.)
12. untamed, between 2 hills or mountains? (wild lily-of-the-valley.)
13. a ferocious cat? (tiger lily.)
14. the Christmas star? (star-of-Bethlehem.)
15. small + light + 3 + small intestine? (dwarf white trillium.)

177. Theme Match

Match the theme with the title of the fiction book.

1. *The Witch of Blackbird Pond* (Speare.) __D__
2. *The Outsiders* (Hinton.) __F__
3. *Julie of the Wolves* (George.) __H__
4. *The Pearl* (Steinbeck.) __B__
5. *The Red Badge of Courage* (Crane.) __J__
6. *Jacob Have I Loved* (Paterson.) __I__
7. *The Pigman* (Zindel.) __C__
8. *My Brother Sam Is Dead* (Collier.) __G__
9. *The Contender* (Lipsyte.) __A__
10. *Sounder* (Armstrong.) __E__

A. courage, identity, friendship, decisions, process of becoming.
B. knowledge versus ignorance, values, good versus evil, pride, greed.
C. communication, responsibility, the importance of human contact, death.
D. prejudice & persecution, friendship, independence, love, adjustment to change.
E. prejudice, courage, loneliness, love, perseverance.
F. socioeconomic conflict, search for self, loyalty, peer relationships, poverty, sacrifice.
G. growing up, family conflict, futility of war, loyalty, justice.
H. courage, the conflict of nature versus civilization,

survival, significance of wild animals and wilderness.
I. family, relationships, growing up, self-worth.
J. importance of self-awareness, courage, fear, war, initiation.

178. Authors Rhyme

What author's name rhymes with:

1. fern? (Verne.)
2. the card game poker? (Stoker.)
3. vain? (Twain.)
4. ring? (King.)
5. Havana? (Cavanna.)
6. mine? (Klein.)
7. bolts? (Stolz.)
8. scat? (Platt.)
9. skull? (Hull.)
10. mall? (Hall.)
11. kindle? (Zindel.)
12. packs? (Sachs.)
13. pink? (Brink.)
14. vixen? (Dixon.)
15. misty? (Christie.)

179. Dark Forces

Answer the following with the title of a supernatural fiction book.

1. how to bring home the groceries? (*Carrie* – King.)
2. hysterical fantasy reverie? (*Fevre Dream* – Martin.)
3. a signal, plus a boy's name? (*Cujo* – King.)
4. phantom builder? (*Ghost-maker* – Kilgore.)
5. evening change? (*Night Shift* – King.)
6. a clowning primate's hand? (*Monkey's Paw* – Richardson.)
7. two times scorched? (*Twice Burned* – Gettel.)
8. where to put dead animals? (*Pet Sematary* – King.)

9. flame initiator? (*Firestarter* — King.)
10. home of murkiness? (*House of Shadows* — Norton.)
11. the lifeless region? (*The Dead Zone* — King.)
12. down a shadowy corridor? (*Down a Dark Hall* — Duncan.)
13. a present? (*Gift* — Dickinson.)
14. the sister of Mr. Ghost? (*Miss Ghost* — Arthur.)
15. an observer in the forest? (*A Watcher in the Woods* — Randall.)

180. Worthy Writer

Answer the following with the name of an author.

1. president of a country? (King.)
2. capital of England? (London.)
3. name of a famous comet? (Haley.)
4. tough plants that survive? (Hardy.)
5. a brand of corn flakes? (Kellogg.)
6. dismal and bleak? (Gray.)
7. a sport of pursuing animals? (Hunt.)
8. the edge? (Brink.)
9. to capture a whale? (Speare.)
10. openings in fences? (Gates.)
11. an iron alloy containing carbon? (Steele.)
12. Jackie Gleason's sidekick in "The Honeymooners"? (Norton.)
13. a type of vacuum cleaner? (Hoover.)
14. an abbreviation for audiovisual? (Avi.)
15. comes from trees? (Wood.)

181. Library Skills Crossword

Across

1. the class number and author letter found on the spine of the book, and in the upper left-hand corner of the catalog card.
3. the index to the library's book collection.
7. subjects contained in a book listed alphabetically,

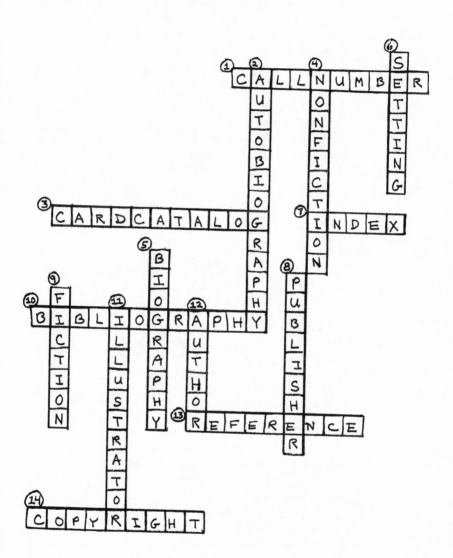

usually found in the last part of the book.
10. a list of books on a special subject.
13. fact-containing books to be used in the library only.
14. tells you if your books contain recent information.

Down

2. a book about the writer's own life.
4. books dealing with factual material.
5. a book about a famous person's life.
6. where the story takes place.
8. prints and distributes the books.
9. books created from an author's imagination.
11. the artist who makes the pictures.
12. person who writes a book.

182. Fiction Author Crossword

Across

1. Author of *Adam of the Road*.
3. Author of *Sugaring Time*.
4. Author of *The Witch of Blackbird Pond*.
6. Author of *Secret of the Andes*.
7. Author of *Up a Road Slowly*.
9. Author of *Young Fu of the Upper Yangtze*.
14. Author of *White Stag*.
15. Author of *Waterless Mountain*.
17. Author of *Hurry Home, Candy*.
18. Author of *Dragonwings*.
19. Author of *And Now Miguel*.

Down

2. Author of *Amos Fortune, Free Man*.
5. Author of *Thimble Summer*.
6. Author of *Dark Is Rising*.
8. Author of *I, Juan De Pareja*.
10. Author of *Carry On, Mr. Bowditch*.
11. Author of *Caddie Woodlawn*.
12. Author of *Gathering of Days*.
13. Author of *Ginger Pye*.
16. Author of *Westing Game*.
20. Author of *Call It Courage*.
21. Author of *Summer of the Swans*.

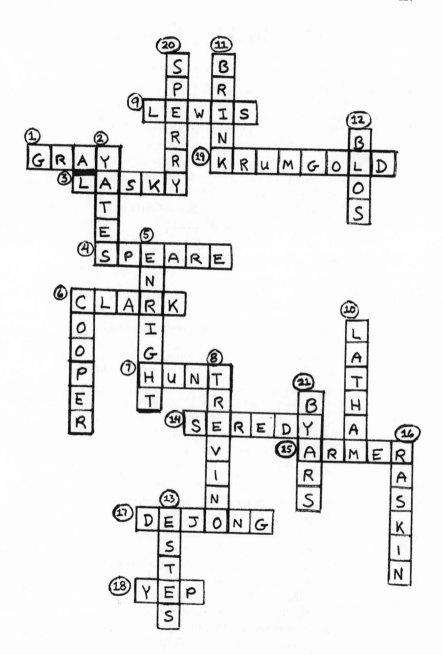

183. Double Meaning

Produce a fiction title with the following words by giving a homonym of the word.

1. born? (*Bourne Identity* — Ludlum.)
2. able? (*Abel's Island* — Steig.)
3. bow? (*Bronze Bow* — Speare.)
4. pie? (*Ginger Pye* — Estes.)
5. see? (*The Old Man and the Sea* — Hemingway.)
6. be? (*Bee* — Cohen.)
7. son? (*Evil Under the Sun* — Christie.)
8. air? (*Jane Eyre* — Brontë.)
9. bare? (*The Teddy Bear Habit* — Collier.)
10. bead? (*Adam Bede* — Eliot.)

184. Authors' Initials

Name an author whose initials begin the words:

1. juicy babble. (Judy Blume.)
2. jubilant rowdy rare tale. (J.R.R. Tolkien.)
3. paramount zealot. (Paul Zindel.)
4. magnificent storyteller. (Mary Stolz.)
5. perfect wisdom. (Phyllis Wood.)
6. bubbling counselor. (Betty Cavanna.)
7. knavish philosopher. (Kin Platt.)
8. scintillating overview. (Scott O'Dell.)
9. magical language. (Madeleine L'Engle.)
10. interesting hogwash. (Irene Hunt.)
11. astute narrator. (Andre Norton.)
12. convincing killjoy. (Carolyn Keene.)
13. scary killer. (Stephen King.)
14. candid scribe lesson. (C.S. Lewis.)
15. ebullient news. (Emily Neville.)
16. self-assured epic. (Sylvia Engdahl.)
17. justifiable gabble. (Jean George.)
18. remarkable scuttlebutt. (Rosemary Sutcliff.)
19. joyous veteran. (Jules Verne.)
20. loquacious wonder. (Laura Wilder.)

185. "G" Game

All these words begin with G.
What is a . . .

1. two-letter word meaning to proceed? (go.)
2. three-letter word meaning to obtain? (get.)
3. four-letter word meaning joy? (glee.)
4. five-letter word meaning polish or luster? (glaze, gloss.)
5. six-letter word meaning sad? (gloomy.)
6. seven-letter word meaning sparkle? (glimmer.)
7. eight-letter word meaning virtue or honesty? (goodness.)
8. nine-letter word meaning impressive? (grandiose.)
9. ten-letter word meaning foundation? (groundwork.)
10. eleven-letter word meaning attraction? (gravitation.)
11. twelve-letter word meaning gibberish? (gobbledygook.)
12. thirteen-letter word meaning bombastic? (grandiloquent.)
13. fourteen-letter word (hint: hyphenated) meaning useless? (good-for-nothing.)

186. Cat Game

Name the following "cats."

1. a domesticated carnivore, a pet. (cat.)
2. something used to locate books. (catalogue.)
3. raft with several logs lashed together. (catamaran.)
4. an abnormality of the eye. (cataract.)
5. a chemical change by addition of a substance. (catalysis.)
6. an underground cemetery. (catacomb.)
7. violent upheaval. (cataclysm.)
8. ancient military engine for throwing darts and stones. (catapult.)

9. a sudden disaster. (catastrophe.)
10. a prefix meaning "down," "against." (cata.)

187. Oh, Henry

How many short stories can you find by O. Henry? Circle each title across, down, or diagonally.

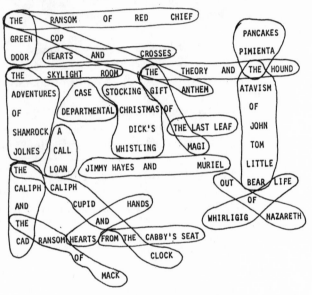

188. Poe's Pallor

Find Edgar Allan Poe's short stories and circle them.

Silence. This is *a tale of the ragged mountains. William Wilson, Ligeia,* and *Eleonora* of *Metzengerstein* all remember *the masque of the red death* and *the fall of the house of usher.* On *the island of the fay,* near *landor's cottage* was *the premature burial* in *the oblong box.* During an instant *loss of breath* in *the conversation of Eiros and Charmion, Berenice* and *the man of the crowd* saw a *shadow* of a *hop-frog.* As to *the colloquy of Monos and Una,* and *the tell-tale heart* of *King Pest, the gold-bug, the black cat, the elk* and *the sphinx* living in *the domain of Arnheim* discovered *the spectacles* of *the murders in the Rue Morgue. Morella, X-ing a paragrab, the imp of the perverse, mellonta tauta* read *the purloined letter, Ms found in a bottle,* a *bon-bon, the assignation,* and *the oval portrait.* "*Thou art the man*," she said. *The devil in the Belfry* explains *the mystery of Marie Roget* and *the balloon hoax* in *the facts in the case of M. Valdemar.* After *a descent into the maelstrom, the cask of Amontillado* was found and *the thousand-and-second tale of Scheherazade* was found in *the pit and the pendulum.*

189. Literary Lore

Name the teenage contemporary fiction title by Betty Cavanna.

1. dance craze? (*Ballet Fever.*)
2. grasp money and lane? (*Catchpenny Street.*)
3. fascination on scrutiny? (*Romance on Trial.*)
4. stomp once and once again for slaughter? (*Stamp Twice for Murder.*)
5. approximately similar to siblings? (*Almost Like Sisters.*)
6. getting toward fourteen plus two? (*Going on Sixteen.*)
7. desired, a female for the steeds? (*Wanted, a Girl for the Horses.*)
8. flounces and percussion? (*Ruffles and Drums.*)
9. one can't bring a score of pets on a rendezvous? (*You Can't Take Twenty Dogs on a Date.*)
10. male at the nearest access? (*Boy Next Door.*)

190. Tree Farm

Name the tree.

1. United States + rhymes with dew? (American yew.)
2. hairless evergreen symbol of mourning? (bald cypress.)
3. a ruddy evergreen with a neat appearance? (red spruce.)

4. a romantic Christmas evergreen? (balsam fir.)
5. higher than a hill + conifer? (mountain pine.)
6. a Halloween gourd + remains? (pumpkin ash.)
7. a place for swimming in summer? (beech.)
8. linden + xylem? (basswood.)
9. canine + xylem? (dogwood.)
10. edge of a skirt + a bolt or fastening part of a door? (hemlock.)
11. rhymes with coke? (oak.)
12. fumes + arbor? (smoketree.)
13. arbor of paradise? (tree-of-heaven.)
14. distasteful lily? (yucca.)
15. wind instrument + crawler? (trumpet creeper.)
16. sugary chewy rubber? (sweetgum.)
17. sparkly gray ringing arbor? (silverbell tree.)

Part VII
Displays, Projects and Exhibits

191. Romance Rap

Display as many romance books as possible. Compile a bibliography of what is available in your library. Decorate with hearts and arrows. Advertise for a group of students who would like to have a discussion session on romance books that they have read. Girls especially are avid readers of romance, and can't wait to get their hands on more titles. Schedule a rap session.

192. Project Week

With the cooperation of the science teacher, exhibit science projects in the library. Our most recent display featured the space program's history and accomplishments to date. Students are very much interested in viewing the work of fellow students.

Likewise, have a math fair week; or a book report model-diorama display week (or make it 2 weeks). Displays in our library often attract children to come in after school to see someone's project.

193. Panoramas of the Past

History or social studies classes may model famous events in history into dioramas. A list of the events is displayed, and student patrons must decide what each scene represents. Models may be made from a mixture of 2 parts flour, 1 part water and a dash of salt (mix with a stick or spoon). Use paints to decorate, and an acrylic spray or even hair spray for a protective finish.

194. Tangram Thingamajigs

Wonderful for the math class! Tangrams are geometric shapes organized to build designs. A tangram includes two large triangles, one medium-sized triangle, two small triangles, a square, and a rhomboid (see figure below). The geometric shapes can be arranged to design one large triangle, square, rectangle, etc. Each student may design an object of his choice: a sailboat, an animal, a car, etc. Display these in the library. The library media specialist may pick the most original and unique tangram.

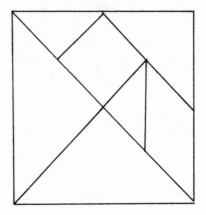

195. Origami Oglio

Origami is the art of paper folding. In connection with the math department, display origami projects in the library. Numerous themes may be incorporated, for instance, animal shapes or flower shapes.

196. Flower Show

Hold a flower show in the library during late March or early April. Plant seeds or bulbs ahead of time so that flowers can be on display at this time. Bring in any flowering plants from home, and invite students to do the same. Have at least 15–20 flowers and flowering plants or shrubs available. Some possibilities are amaryllis, forsythia, narcissus, violets, hyacinths, Easter lilies, tulips, crocuses, daffodils, begonias, cyclamen, jonquils, snowdrops, garlic, and chives.

197. Remedial Hobby Yak

The remedial group or the emotionally disturbed or learning disabled students may or may not like coming to the library. I have found that some of them love coming, and checking out books. Hold a hobby fair or special interest session with them. Ask them to bring in their hobbies to be displayed. If they are unable to do so because of the hobby's size, ask them to take a picture of it (for example, motorcycles). Show them books on their interests, using both reference and general collection materials. Hold a rap session, and have an exhibition of plenty of materials. You may be surprised at how often these students will come back to the library.

198. Get High on Reading

As each pupil reads a fiction book, his/her name is placed on a balloon made of construction paper. These are placed in the school hallways.

199. Grinches and Goofers

Students who have a book overdue for at least a week or more in the library are categorized in the main hallway. A funny-looking picture may head the caption:

Grinches	Goonies	Goofers
Over 2 weeks	2 weeks	1 week

Students hopefully will not see their names under these captions! A list may also be read over the radio announcements.

200. Book-of-the-Month

Feature a particular fiction book each month of the school year — for example, *Dicey's Song* by Cynthia Voigt. Display the book in a "Book Review Corner." Exhibit a synopsis of the book, and comments written by students about the book. Also display other books by this author such as *Building Blocks; Callender Papers; Homecoming; Runner; Solitary Blue; Tell Me If the Lovers Are Losers.*

201. Vertical File

Display pamphlets, folders, and materials from the vertical file. Place these in a special rack so that students will be aware that such material is available to them.

Index

Numbers refer to game numbers rather than to pages.